SMILE WITH ME

Stephen J. Skubik, CLU and Lois Dutton

THE NATIONAL UNDERWRITER COMPANY
CINCINNATI, OHIO

Library of Congress Catalogue Card Number: 80-84695
ISBN 0-87218-014-X

FOREWORD

Most people know the insurance business is a large industry that performs a very important function. But I doubt that many are aware of the challenges, the trials, or the great personal satisfaction that insurance people experience in the course of their work. Or how much fun they have.

Insurance is a business filled with first-rate men and women who earn their living by performing a wide variety of services for people from all walks of life. They counsel them on their financial security needs, design insurance programs for them, collect premiums from them, pay their claims, tend to their grievances. And out of this rich and varied experience has grown a distinctive body of humor and funny stories, some true and others wildly exaggerated or entirely fanciful.

There are the jokes that agents love to tell about the triumphs and tribulations of fellow agents. Like the one about the new agent who sold a life insurance policy to a 93-year-old man. "I know I said everybody is a good prospect," thundered the agent's sales manager, "but what made you sign up a 93-year-old man?" "Boss, this guy is a good risk," the young agent insisted. "I looked up the figures, and very few people die at that age."

There are the bizarre claims that every insurance company receives. For instance, the one from the unfortunate gentleman afflicted with "walking ammonia." Or the woman suffering from "very close veins."

There are the stories about the complaints that sometimes come in. Like the one from the backwoods mother of seven who wrote asking her company to quit sending premium notices on her husband's life insurance policy.

"He passed away four years ago," she explained, "and I can't afford to keep up the premiums any longer."

There are the gags about the arcane ways of our actuaries, men and women whose sophisticated skills are as vital to our business as those of the engineer are to aeronautics. At Prudential, our actuaries constantly poke fun at themselves in a newsletter famous for its irreverence. Actuaries, one issue explained, are people who would rather be completely wrong than approximately right.

Many jokes and cartoons have been inspired by Prudential's famous Rock of Gibraltar symbol. For example, when Queen Elizabeth II visited Gibraltar some years ago, a New Jersey newspaper printed a cartoon that showed her receiving assurances from an aide as she was about to ascend the famous Rock. "There's no cause for alarm, your Majesty," the aide was saying. "It's as safe as the Prudential."

Our "piece of the rock" slogan has become part of the American vernacular and is the source of the countless quips. One of them was the line Bob Hope used to open a Christmas television show from the rocky island of Okinawa: "So this is what my Prudential agent was talking about when he said I should get a piece of the rock."

Then there's the one about — but the funny stories about our business are legion, as the ensuing pages will indicate. I am delighted that Stephen Skubik, Lois Dutton, and *The National Underwriter Company* have collaborated to produce this delightful book, which will allow readers both within and outside the industry to enjoy a very human side of a wonderful business.

> Robert A. Beck, CLU
> Chairman and Chief Executive Officer
> Prudential Insurance Company of America

Stephen J. Skubik, CLU

Mr. Skubik has been in the insurance business for 27 years, all with Prudential Insurance of America, and is the manager of his company's brokerage office in Washington, D.C.

He has been interested in politics and became a founding board member and national executive director of the Life Underwriters Political Action Committee (LUPAC). In the "District" insurance circles he has been very active having been president of the CLU chapter, a CLU teacher for 11 years and has served on the boards of GAMA and the life underwriters.

Writing is an avocation of Mr. Skubik. In addition to editing three books on humor, *Politics Is Fun, Handbook of Humor By Famous Politicians* and *Republican Humor,* he has written newsletters for insurance and political fields, political pamphlets, and published poetry.

Mr. Skubik is vice president of the Beethoven Institute of Music, collector of icons and curator of the Icon Foundation. In World War II he was in the Counter Intelligence Corps (CIC).

Lois Dutton

Miss Dutton has unique credentials.

She is a concert cellist. She has been a language instructor with Berlitz International School (lived in Europe for eight years and speaks German and Dutch fluently). She has organized medical congresses and symposia. She's a teacher and the Bible, philosophy, tennis for beginners, swimming, lifesaving, piano and cello are her areas of skill and interest.

Her hobbies include public speaking, writing, music, opera, drama, and literature with special interest in Shakespeare and Mark Twain. She loves humor and enjoys making people laugh.

Marketing is her field. She now lives in Keene, New Hampshire, was educated at Covenant College and American University, and has completed her studies in philosophy at Het Vrij Universitat, Amsterdam, The Netherlands.

ACKNOWLEDGEMENTS

Lois Dutton suggested to me, Steve Skubik, that we co-author a book on insurance humor. Such a book could show that the insurance business can have its fun side even though it is a serious business which helps many people avoid economic disaster. It has been a pleasure to receive and read the hundreds of fun-packed stories sent to us from all over the United States.

We wisk to thank the more than one hundred persons in the insurance business who took time from their busy schedules to help us put together the first book ever to be published on insurance humor.

Price Gaines, CLU, RHU, Editor of Life and Health Publications for The National Underwriter Company, was most encouraging. He deserves a great deal of credit for making this book possible. We thank him.

Our sincerest thanks to Austin R. Adkinson, Executive Director, Life Underwriters Political Action Committee, for his cooperation.

We are grateful to Sam P. Gaglio, CLU, Editor and Business Manager, *Life Association News,* for his advice on how to proceed to get the material, especially the cartoons from *Life Association News.*

Also, our various friends at Prudential Insurance Company of America deserve our heartfelt thanks. Bob Beck, CLU, Chairman and Chief Executive Officer of Prudential, took time out of his busy schedule to help. Gloria Molskness, a Prudential gem of a secretary, helped with the typing. Thanks Gloria.

We couldn't have produced this book without the help, cooperation and encouragement of our friends. Thanks a million.

Lois Dutton   Steve Skubik

INTRODUCTION

Henry David Thoreau wrote, "If misery loves company, misery has company enough." "Never save a smile for the right moment. Spend your smiles lavishly. The moment is always right for a smile," said Frank Tyger. The great American wit, Mark Twain said, "The best way to cheer yourself is to try to cheer somebody else up." And Ralph Waldo Emerson said, "It is a happy talent to know how to play."

We know that humor is a special gift from God. He gave us the ability to laugh, to be cheerful, to smile. Human beings are God's highest creation in the animal kingdom. No other kind of animal is capable of smiling. "Laugh and the world laughs with you, weep and you weep alone." And as Thomas Fuller said, "Sorrow is good for nothing but sin."

During Abraham Lincoln's trip to Gettysburg he contracted a highly contagious fever. However, that did not stop the favor seekers who insisted on seeing him. "Let them come in," said Lincoln to his appointment secretary, "at last I have something I can give everyone."

Since there are so many reasons for insurance people to be grouchy, especially the insurance salesperson who failed to make "the" sale, we thought we would give you a book that presents the fun side of the insurance business.

We hope that you find a story or two in this book which will cheer you and that you will make use of some of the stories to bring laughter to others. Be of good cheer: enjoy yourself. God gave you a most wonderful gift when He gave you your beautiful smile. SO SMILE! We dare you.

LIST OF CONTRIBUTORS

We wish to thank the following people for the stories you are about to read. Without them this book would not have been possible.

Gene Akin, CLU, Lubbock, Texas
A.L. Balfay, CLU, Tyler, Texas
Margaret R. Beck, Redding, California
Jack Boyer, Montesano, Washington
Frank J. Brennan, CLU, Jacksonville, Florida
Barbara A. Brown, Annapolis, Maryland
Roger A. Brownell, Santa Barbara, California
John T. Carpenter, III, Columbia, So. Carolina
John R. Carter, New Providence, Pennsylvania
Kenneth B. Cohen, Maryland Heights, Missouri
Anthony T. Colombo, Rochester, New York
Mark S. Coppock, Albany, Georgia
George A. Corkum, CLU, Ft. Lauderdale, Florida
David L. Corrie, Nowhere, Alaska
Catherine Covey, Rochester, New York
Ernest E. Cragg, CLU, Evanston, Illinois
B. Leonard Critcher, CLU, Shreveport, Louisiana
Thomas A. Crowe, Logansport, Indiana
Charles Crumbly, Laurel, Mississippi
James S. Doyle, CLU, Cincinnati, Ohio
J. David Dukehart, CLU, Oakland, California
Tom Fitzgerald, St. Louis, Missouri
Maurice S. Gilbert, Rockville, Maryland
Sid Gleason, Columbia, So. Carolina
Meryl R. Grayer, CLU, New York, New York
James E. Griffith, CLU, Wilmington, Delaware
Clifford C. Halfhill, CLU, Tacoma, Washington
Harry L. Hamilton, CLU, Ft. Lauderdale, Florida
Joseph T. Hanlon, White Plains, New York

Gene Hanson, CLU, Corvallis, Oregon
John C. Hargrave, CLU, La Porte, Indiana
Jerry A. Herzberg, CLU, Tulsa, Oklahoma
Vernon W. Holleman, CLU, Washington, D.C.
E.L. (Jim) Horton, Charlotte, No. Carolina
Phil Irby, Jr., CLU, Jackson, Mississippi
Bower L. Johnston, Jackson, Mississippi
Thomas C. Karrasch, CLU, Roanoke, Virginia
Lawrence G. Katz, CLU, Houston, Texas
Howard O. Kemper, Phoenix, Arizona
Raymond E. King, Jr., CLU, Ft. Wayne, Indiana
Jerome H. Kohn, CLU, Billings, Montana
Murray W. Kronick, CLU, Rockville, Maryland
Jerry Larson, Highland, Indiana
Norman G. Levine, CLU, San Francisco, California
Annemarie Maier, Newark, New Jersey
Melvin L. Maisel, White Plains, New York
Managers Magazine, LIMRA, Hartford, Connecticut
Thomas J. McInerney, CLU, Kingston, New York
Patricia A. McMahon, Alexandria, Minnesota
Morland G. McManigal, CLU, CPCU, Fairfield,
     California
Jennie L. McNulty, Melbourne, Florida
Richard D. Mead, CLU, Scottsbluff, Nebraska
Carl E. Meyering, MBE, Detroit, Michigan
Edward J. Mintz, CLU, Palo Alto, California
A.B. Mirmelstein, Dallas, Texas
Herbert F. Mischke, CLU, St. Paul, Minnesota
Raymond P. Nash, CLU, Adrian, Michigan
Frank Nathan, CLU, Beverly Hills, California
Bright Newhouse, Clarendon, Texas
Charles D. Nord, CLU, Nashville, Tennessee
Lawrence J. O'Brien, Washington, D.C.
J.R. Pegues, Jr., CLU, Tupelo, Mississippi
Larry D. Petty, CLU, Rockford, Illinois
Gene Prosser, Jerseyville, Illinois
Theodore M. Provenza, Timonium, Maryland
Ellen M. Putnam, CLU, Rochester, New York
Russell C. Reitz, CLU, Williamsport, Pennsylvania
Ross Rennie, Newark, New Jersey

Clifton H. Robertson, Richmond, Virginia
Sumner Rodman, CLU, Chestnut Hill, Massachusetts
Robert L. Rose, CLU, Washington, D.C.
Carl B. Rush, CLU, Ft. Wayne, Indiana
Ruth Russell, CLU, North Vernon, Indiana
Fred J. Schubert, CLU, Houston, Texas
Ken Schweiger, Los Angeles, California
Eleanor J. Sivillo, Erie, Pennsylvania
Stephen J. Skubik, CLU, Washington, D.C.
Jerry Stahmer, CLU, Denver Colorado
Vern Strubble, Corvallis, Oregon
Patricia R. Taylor, Mobile, Alabama
Laverne Terry, Newark, New Jersey
John O. Todd, CLU, Evanston, Illinois
Gerald D. Tucker, CLU, Aberdeen Township, New
    Jersey
Martin D. Vogt, Ft. Washington, Pennsylvania
J. Sam Warren, CLU, Macon, Georgia
F. Grice Whiteley, CLU, Charlottesville, Virginia
Jack M. Williams, CLU, Oklahoma City, Oklahoma
Patrick V. Wippel, CLU, Lancaster, Pennsylvania
Marshall L. Wolper, CLU, Miami, Florida
R. Edwin Wood, CLU, San Francisco, California
Jack Woods, Billings, Montana
John L. Wozniak, CLU, Missoula, Montana
Bart Yohn, Newark, New Jersey
Lewis C. Yount, CLU, Seattle, Washington

"Thank you for your invitation to participate as a contributor to your insurance humor book. However, I have never found anything funny about insurance. Know lots of funny true stories about people in the insurance business... but those are not repeatable!"

Meryl R. Grayer, CLU

Please Refer to ...

I called on a doctor/administrator for one of our hospitals. He was interested but said his wife was opposed to putting any money in life insurance because it was such a poor investment. I suggested I go see her. He called his wife and said I was coming over. She was a large woman. As soon as I got in the house she told me they did not want any life insurance. I explained the plan I had discussed with her husband but still she was adamant that they neither needed nor wanted life insurance.

Then I admired her house, her furniture and her decorations. Then she offered me a cup of tea and some cookies which, I said, were delicious. We talked about recipes and I copied many of them, discussed menus, etc. Finally, she said, "Now, just tell me more about this plan you have."

I went over the presentation carefully. Without a word, she grabbed the telephone, called her husband and said in an accusing voice, "Why haven't you taken this $20,000 policy Miss Putnam worked out for us?" The policy was placed and kept in force until it became a death claim years later.

— Ellen M. Putnam, CLU

When I was new in the business, early in 1957, I made daytime calls on housewives to acquire evening appointments with their husbands so I could sell mortgage protection insurance. Cold convassing.

One day, while working in a new, modest income development, I acquired a 6:30 pm appointment with a young couple from Alabama, who had recently moved to Fort Lauderdale. The husband was employed as a drag line operator.

As I drove up, following one of our summer gully-washer thunderstorms, I saw the husband waiting in the carport; usually not a good sign. He stood 6'3" and weighed in around 250 pounds.

My first thought was, "I hope he's not unhappy about this appointment." So, seeing him there as I pulled-up, I waved and nodded my head.

As I got out of my car, I stepped right into a huge pot-hole filled with water to the level of the pavement. Losing my balance, I did a one-and-a-half, backward-twisting, head-first plunge into a muddy drainage ditch, which ran through his front yard. Before I realized what had happened, I was in two to three feet of muddy water, totally submerged at first. Then sitting there, with my head just out of the water, I groped for my glasses and the proposal.

I tried to scramble up the bank, out of the ditch, but the sides were just too slick. I kept sliding back down into the water and my shoes were getting stuck in the mud.

By now, you might expect my prospect to be rolling on the ground, laughing hysterically, but he wasn't. Seeing my plight, he came charging down his driveway with a bath towel he grabbed off a wash line. He held it out to me so I could climb up. I think he believed I was going to drown or disappear into the mud, right in his front yard.

After reaching the hard pavement, I stood there, soaked to the skin, muddy beyond belief, in what had been a light blue, Palm Beach suit. He motioned me towards the carport where he hosed me down. After this, I figured, he would dismiss me so he could go tell someone about his clutzy insurance man. I was wrong again!

Finally, he spoke to me suggesting that I go into his utility room and get out of my clothes. Soon, he was back with his bathrobe and all my clothes were in his washer.

There I was — in his bathrobe, still a little grimy, my muddy proposal in hand at his kitchen table. I went through my presentation and he bought the insurance policy with hardly a question.

Later, we chatted over coffee while my clothes dried. Then, and only then, did he show any amusement over my swan dive into his drainage ditch.

That night, as I drove home in my rumpled suit, I laughed so hard at times that my eyes filled with tears and I couldn't see to drive. My new client showed nothing but compassion and concern. It was a marvelous experience under the most difficult circumstances and will always be my most unforgettable sale.

— *George A. Corkum, CLU*

When I first entered the insurance business, I was very timid, shy and frightened. One of my first interviews was with a referral whom I had never met and who sounded quite gruff on the telephone. My general agent agreed to go with me on the interview.

It was a sultry night, and as we approached the home of my prospect, I was getting very uptight. My general agent said to me, "If you run into trouble, just turn to me and say 'What do you think of that, Mr. Gruber?', and I will take over the interview." I now felt very relieved because I knew my general agent would be there to back me up.

We approached the door, and I rang the doorbell. After a very brief wait, the door opened and I was confronted by this huge man in a T-shirt, a can of beer in one hand and the other hand on the door. He said in a loud, gruff voice, "Wadda ya want?" I immediately replied, "What do you think of that, Mr. Gruber?"

— *Gerald D. Tucker, CLU*

On a recent European trip I introduced Ben Feldman to a very pretty German girl guide. I took a photo of the two together with Ben's arm around her waist. Returning to California, I called on a client who told me that his partner in Cleveland insisted on doing business with Ben Feldman. I called Ben and told him I had this incriminating picture of him and the German girl that I would expose to the world unless he split the case with me. He laughingly agreed.

I sent him the photo. He told me it enhanced his reputation with his sons.

— *Edward J. Mintz, CLU*

I always trained new agents to throw the ball to me — if a question or objection came-up during an interview. They would simply turn to me and say, "How

LIFE ASSOCIATION NEWS

"The pay and fringe benefits are satisfactory, but what can we work out about my showing up for work on that dull, drab day called Monday?"

4

about that, Mr. Corkum?" Having thus trained a new, middle-aged salesman, we went to make some calls just to acquire an appointment.

As we approached the first house, Ed said to me, "Let me handle this one." He confidently pressed the door bell, stepped back, cleared his throat, adjusted his tie, and as the lady of the house appeared, he boomed out, "Good morning, my name is Ed Holmes." Then, as if struck deaf, dumb, and blind, his mind went completely blank.

He gulped, paled, and began to sweat profusely. I didn't know what to do, and the lady glared back at the both of us. Finally, he looked right at me and said, "Ain't that right, Mr. Corkum?" with a hugh sigh of relief.

I couldn't contain myself. I quickly replied, "That's right, you are Ed Holmes and it is a good morning."

FASHIONS FOR
THE WOMAN
ON HER WAY UP!

LIFE ASSOCIATION NEWS

"Something in an executive vice president range. I wouldn't want the personnel director to think I'm overdressed!"

And then I cracked up. He did too, realizing what he had done. The door was then slammed in our faces, and we retreated, laughing and bumping into each other. As I approached the car, I caught a glimpse of a very concerned lady peering out of the window at us.

Later, that same agent became very successful and opened his own shop. Whenever we meet now, he always says, "Ain't that right, Mr. Corkum?" And I always reply, "That's right, you are Ed Holmes, and it is indeed a very good day." As we both get hysterical, people around us wonder what in the hell is so funny about that.

— *George A. Corkum, CLU*

As a member of the Rochester Chapter of the American Chemical Society, I knew many of the Chemists in several of the scientific manufacturing companies and wrote quite a bit of business with one company. From one client I was referred to another executive, a small, pleasant man who wanted me to talk with him and his wife. I went to their house one evening and met his wife, a large, domineering woman. To introduce me her husband pleasantly said, "I told Miss Putnam that you had relatives by the name of Putnam." Her answer was, "Well, they didn't amount to much." I sold a small policy for one of their sons. Later we became good friends.

— *Ellen M. Putnaum, CLU*

"I got some great referral leads today," said the first agent.

"I didn't sell any business, either," said the second.

— *Jennie Larson McNulty*

Early in my insurance career, I had a client and friend who provided me with names of suspects for insurance sales. One day she gave me the name of a friend whose husband didn't believe in life insurance and, of course, didn't have any coverage. I made contact with the prospect and set-up an appointment for 7:30 one evening.

I had been out of town all day on the day of our appointment and had not eaten before arriving back in town. Knowing the man was a Dane, who loved to drink coffee and eat fine pastries, I decided to stop at a bakery for some delicious cinnamon rolls to take with me.

When I knocked on the prospect's door, he greeted me with, "Didn't you get the message that I had called and we have decided not to buy any insurance?" I replied that I had just arrived back in town and hadn't checked with the answering service, but that I had brought some tasty rolls, and if he would provide some coffee, we could share them together.

He invited me in and we visited while his lovely wife made some coffee. We discussed everything but life insurance. Finally, he said, "Well, what about this life insurance, anyway?" I presented several ideas to him that fit his situation and after answering several of his questions, he said, "That sure isn't the way I thought it was. I'll take that number two plan." That plan was for $10,000 and an annual premium of $357. This wasn't a big deal for some, but for him it was a major undertaking.

In succeeding years, I wrote several more policies on him and his wife. Whenever I made an appointment with him, he always said, "Be sure to bring some more cinnamon rolls!"

— *Gene Hansen, CLU*

I called on a referred lead one time and met with a lady who seemed to be in her early forties. While I was visiting with her a young man, who appeared to be in his early twenties, entered the room. I was introduced to

7

him and, after the usual pleasantries, I asked the lady if she had some life insurance on her son. She replied, "That is my husband." I didn't make a sale.

— Gene Akin, CLU

LIFE ASSOCIATION NEWS

"Miss Bettis, we insist you say 'Sappenstein, Appery, Penmeiner and Silverberg' every time you answer the phone instead of abbreviating it to SAPS!"

"I Object!"

Agent Pippins was a great salesman of retirement insurance. Once he was up against a very tough prospect so, as a last resort, Pippins pulled his secret weapon out of his arsenal. This persuasive point was his very own and he didn't know any other insurance agent who used it. But it always worked for him.

"Mr. McGee, in addition to the security and carefree days this plan will give you in your golden years, there is one more advantage for you. There will be more women around than men. In fact, at age 75, there are 18% more women than men, How about that, Mr. McGee?"

Mr. McGee looked our agent straight in the eyes and said," At age 75, who cares?"

— *Ken Schweiger*

LIFE ASSOCIATION NEWS

"Your last educated guess cost me $1,500!"

The businessman had just signed up for another $25,000 policy on his life. He turned to the agent and said, "Young man, you may well feel proud of yourself. I've refused to see five insurance agents today."

"I know," said the agent, "I'm them."

— *Jennie Larson McNulty*

I was sharing an interview with a rookie agent and the prospect was a cold call. The rookie agent, we'll call him Ron, had been knocking on doors looking for people to talk with and had obtained several appointments. At this point in his career he had no sales experience or product knowledge so the appointments he did make for a couple of weeks were shared by me.

LIFE ASSOCIATION NEWS

During one interview with a young couple who had three youngsters, it came out that the wife had nearly lost her sister in an auto accident.

I went to great lengths to explain the benefits of the life insurance concept; both permanent and term. The husband readily grasped the full concept and said, "Well, I would like to know what a program like this would be for $25,000 that you mentioned and $75,000 decreasing term." I calculated the premium for this coverage and the husband said that was fine; he could afford it.

At this moment the wife stepped in and said, "Wait a minute, I don't understand what's going on here. Just what is it you're talking about?" I immediately went into a picture diagram again to explain exactly what we were talking about, using very simple terms. When I felt that I had explained exactly what her husband wanted to do I asked, "Do you have any further questions or objections?" She replied, "I don't understand any of it, but I don't really care. Just get him to sign the application."

— *Vern Strubble*

Early in my career, I was calling a list of "non-repliers" on a direct mailing... getting all the usual negative responses and rejections when I finally reached a voice that answered "Wrong number, maybe?" This was as close to pleasant that I came to in four hours. We both got a good laugh and he explained he had just gotten his phone and knew no one in Mobile. I responded, "I don't know, you've just made my day."

As a result of his bit of humor in my fruitless day, we set up an appointment and it did result in the sale of two policies.

— *Patricia R. Taylor*

LIFE ASSOCIATION NEWS

"Looks like the rumor that Jones won the state lottery is true."

I was selling insurance to an 18-year-old son of a skinflint farmer. The son was an intelligent young man who knew what he was buying. He had a good job and could afford the insurance which I had proposed. Skinflint was present at the sales interview because I had invited him, as is my practice when selling to juveniles. He was absolutely horrified at the thought of the amount of premium his son would spend to buy $17,000 of Whole Life. The son agreed to buy it. The father objected to the proposal that I made. His final (futile) objection was: "I've had $2,000 of life insurance since I was 26 and I've never got a cent out of it!"

— *Raymond P. Nash, CLU*

While doing joint work with an agent, we acquired an appointment with a lady in a very fashionable neighborhood. After an unsuccessful interview the agent and I returned to his car and proceeded to back out of the driveway — over her mailbox. The woman was watching and we all proceeded to survey the damage. The mailbox lay on the ground, sheared off at the base.

My new agent feebly tried to make amends. However, the woman was irate. As she strode away with the mailbox in her hand, the agent blurted out, "Does that mean you don't want me to come back and explain my mortgage plan to your husband?"

She turned, glared at him and said, "Does it cover stuff like this?" waving the mailbox at him.

"No ma'am," he said, "that's homeowners insurance that pays for stuff like that."

"Do you sell homeowners?", she asked.

"No ma'am," he replied, shaking his head.

"You ought to," she screamed, "you might do better!"

As we drove away I gave way to hysteria. The agent couldn't see the humor in it. Four days later, his wife arrived at my office with all of his supplies. She announced that he was through with insurance sales. The day before he had been bitten by a German Shephard, and later had become sick to his stomach on another lady's front porch (a condition he had quite often, she informed me, when under stress).

As she walked out of the door, she told me she was going home to get him and they were going to where his car had been left the day before, due to a dead battery.

I thought maybe I would quit after a week like that. Fortunately, I never had one like it.

— *George A. Corkum, CLU*

LIFE ASSOCIATION NEWS

". . . And I'll tell you why you're not selling, Johnson, the customers aren't taking you seriously!"

I will never forget my first joint interview. The new agent had learned his interview technique and with enthusiasm made an appointment with the owner of a local cleaning establishment. We met this prospect at his place of business and the new agent placed his interview book on the ironing board and commenced the interview.

About half-way through the interview the prospect reached up, took down a hose and sprayed steam all over the agent's interview book, wilting the pages like lettuce leaves. It was all I could do to keep from laughing. My man said, "Is this not a good time to discuss insurance?" The answer was obvious.

— *Vernon W. Holleman, Jr., CLU*

We Are Now Taking Applications

Upon taking over my new duties in the Lancaster Office I accompanied a relatively new agent, who had been having sales difficulties, on an interview with an elderly couple. After considerable discussion and fact-finding, it developed that there was a possible need for substantial insurance on the prospect. The prospect responded with, "Well, I'm not sure that I want this." In answer, I responded, "I'm not sure that Prudential will be able to get it for you, but we will need a medical exam in order to find out." I said to the agent, "Go ahead and fill out the form so we can get this started for Mr. _____ ." The agent replied, "What form?" I responded quietly to him, "The app, you dummy!" But this did result in a substantial sale for this agent.

— Patrick V. Wipple, CLU

LIFE ASSOCIATION NEWS

"Well, actually, I do try to better myself, sir. But up to now, this company's the best I can do."

17

An agent, writing a policy for a cowpuncher, asked him whether he had ever had any accidents. "No," said the cowboy, "except once a bronc kicked me and another time a rattlesnake bit me."

"Don't you call those accidents?" asked the agent.

"No," replied the cowboy, "they done it on purpose."

— *Managers Magazine*

LIFE ASSOCIATION NEWS

"Don't let the fact you've never worked bother you. Some of our employees still don't!"

On her very first sales interview with a funeral director, my new female recruit began to fill out the application. She asked for his name, his height, and his weight. He gave his name and said he was 5'9" and weighed 175 pounds.

Somehow she felt that that was worthy of a comment and said, "That's a nice size."

— *Larry D. Petty, CLU*

The late Bennet Cerf once told a story of Young Connelly whose father had been hanged as a horse thief. Connelly experienced a little trouble in filling out an application blank for life insurance.

The cause of his mother's death was easy; double pneumonia. It took several minutes, however, before he found the proper words to explain his old man's demise. After thinking, he came up with these words: "My father was taking part in a heavily attended public function when the platform gave way."

— *John C. Hargrave, CLU*

LIFE ASSOCIATION NEWS

"I see you copped out on your last job because you weren't getting enough bread!"

I received a phone call from a woman who said she was interested in buying some life insurance for her daughter's college education. I asked her where she lived and when I could come out to talk with her. She said, "You can come over now, if you are not too busy." I allowed that I was not too busy and that I would be right over. I grabbed my rate book and ran down the street where I hailed a cab. I arrived at her place in less than twenty minutes.

When I got to her apartment, in a very ritzy part of Washington, I knocked on the door. The woman who opened the door was a knockout. She was very beautiful. Her hair was auburn, her skin lily-white, her eyes large and dark, her lips were shaped like a heart and her body was that of Venus. She asked me to come in. I entered the apartment and found it to be very attractively furnished. She was obviously a lady of wealth.

I was directed to sit next to a table in the alcove overlooking a park. She sat down on the other chair and proceeded to explain that she was in a hurry to buy the insurance inasmuch as she was about to leave for Spain. She asked if she could get the insurance policy before she left. I said that it would depend upon how quickly the underwriting department could make a decision. I told her that normally it would take a couple of weeks. She asked if the policy could be mailed to her in Spain. I allowed that it could.

She got up from the table and went to her kitchen and brought out a bottle of liquor and two poney glasses. She poured herself a drink and asked if I cared for one. I accepted the drink. We discussed the need for the insurance and the amount. She told me that she wanted her daughter, who was only seven years old, to have at least $20,000 when she was eighteen. We talked about the cost of college education and that eleven years hence the cost would very likely be higher. She said that she was prepared to pay more if necessary. She then went to her dresser drawer and pulled out $20,000 in cash. She said she would give me the cash for the policy. I couldn't believe my eyes and what I was hearing. I had never had such an easy sale.

I looked into the rate book and decided upon an endowment policy paid-up at age eighteen with all premiums paid in advance. The value in 11 years would be about $30,000. The woman said she was glad to be doing business with a company that had such an intelligent agent as I. Needless to say, I was flattered.

As we discussed the details of the policy, she kept pouring more and more liquor for herself. I nursed my one drink, but she must have had at least ten. I noticed she was getting tipsy and thought that I should get the application signed before she became drunk. I knew that if she was intoxicated, I could not get a valid signature. I asked the questions on the application, and when I came to the question of occupation, she answered, "Countess." I told her that was not an occupation. Could I not just put down "housewife"? She became angry and said that she was not a housewife. I explained that it was merely a way of stating that she was not engaged in any occupation but that she was a woman who took care of her husband and child. In America, I said, we called such a woman a housewife.

By the time I got to explaining the way the question should be answered, she had had a few more drinks and was obviously drunk. She asked for my calling card. It read, "Stephen J. Skubik, Special Agent". She screamed at me, shouting why had I not told her that I was with the FBI. I said that I was not with the FBI, that I was a special agent with my insurance company.

Returning to the application, I still couldn't get her to accept the wording "housewife" to the question of occupation. She was very disturbed. Each time I tried to explain the word, she rejected it. She got so angry that she picked up the liquor bottle and threatened me with it. I decided that I had better get out of her apartment before she hit me. I told her that unless I got a satisfactory answer to the question, I could not submit the application. I continued by saying that she was too drunk to competently respond to the questions and I was prohibited from taking an application on a person who was drunk. She was livid and ordered me to leave. I left and felt very upset at having lost the easy sale.

I went home and related the story to my wife. When I got to the office the next day, I told the story to my manager. He said that I had been too technical, that I should have taken the application and the $20,000 in cash. I had thought that I had done the right thing. I felt badly about all the commissions I had lost and about the reaction of my manager.

That afternoon I got a phone call. It was the Countess. She asked me to come right over, that she was willing to go along with "housewife" on the application. I was thrilled at the prospects of reviving the lost case.

I hurried over to her apartment. When I knocked on the door, the Countess opened it and I couldn't believe my eyes. She was dressed in a sheer negligee and her beautifully shaped body was exciting to see. I entered and noticed that her sofa bed had been laid out and the sheets turned back. She snuggled against me and kissed me on the lips. I was beside myself. I said that I needed to get some air. She laughed and again planted her lips against mine. I pulled back. I asked her, "Would you mind if I smoke a cigar?"

She then told me she had decided to suduce me in order for me to place the application with my company. I told her she needn't do that. I also told her that I was happily married. She said, "Special Agent Stephen, you are a funny man." I allowed that indeed I was a funny man. She asked me if I really didn't know what she did for a living. I replied that I didn't. She told me that if the company knew what she did, they wouldn't issue the policy. So I left again without the application.

I have always wondered what she did for a living which would cause my company not to issue her a policy for the education of her daughter.

— *Stephen J. Skubik, CLU*

Upon entering the agency on a Friday morning several years ago, I overheard a discussion between two agents. It started this way:

"Two?"

"No."

"Three."

"No."

"Four."

"No."

This continued all the way up to eight, before a yes was given. Overjoyed, since the agent being questioned had been doing very poorly, I made a mental resolution to treat the entire agency to lunch because this particular agent had written eight applications during the previous day. Much to my dismay, further inquiry revealed that she hadn't written eight applications, but that her dog had delivered eight puppies the night before.

— *Patrick V. Wippel, CLU*

LIFE ASSOCIATION NEWS

"I'd prefer taking this client golfing—it's tough catching up to him on a ski slope to write up his order!"

The very first month I entered the life insurance business, I sold an annuity to a woman who worked in the Labor Department of the federal government. Her job consisted of helping women find employment. When I submitted the application to the home office I described her job as, "Helping women in labor." you can well imagine the reply I received from the underwriting department!

— *Bob Rose, CLU*

LIFE ASSOCIATION NEWS

"These files contain the names and addresses and personal histories of 34 million Americans we're not interested in."

I was a thirty-seven year old agent of three months' experience and still a little bit shy about asking the spouse the question on the family application, "Are you pregnant?"

During the writing of an application on a 25-year-old Army Lieutenant and his pretty 23-year-old wife, who looked the epitome of saintliness, I inevitably came to the pregnancy question which bothered me and made me feel uneasy. "Mrs. Oliver, are you pregnant?", I asked. Without hesitation and with a little giggle she replied, "Well, I wasn't up until last night, but now I'm not so sure."

Needless to say, in one little statement this young wife had corrected my feeling of wistfulness in aksing the question in future interviews.

— *Sid Gleason*

On the application for employment to become an agent with my insurance company is the question: "Have you ever been arrested?" A prospective recruit answered, "No." The following question was: "Why?" Not realizing the question was meant for those who had replied, "Yes," the recruit answered, "Never got caught."

— *Stephen J. Skubik, CLU*

LIFE ASSOCIATION NEWS

"Well, if it isn't Jerry Barnes from high
school, the guy that always called me a
dumb blonde!"

"Hey, Fella', You Want to Buy ..."

"Her references say she has enough intelligence for two people! She should make a perfect private secretary for the ol'man."

During the close of an interview the prospect's young son, about age five, came into the room. After answering his son's question, the father told him that he was talking business and did not want to be disturbed again. Finally, the young boy walked briskly into the room, put his hands on his hips, looked his father squarely in the eyes and said, "Daddy, when is that guy going home?" After a good laugh, I quickly tried again for a close and succeeded in making a sale.

— *Phil Irby, Jr., CLU*

I called a prospect, Mr. Johnson, who said to come out any day between 2:00 and 5:00 pm. When I reached the receptionist I saw out of the corner of my eye Mr. Johnson talking with an agent whom I knew. So, I told the receptionist I wanted to see Mr. Williams, not knowing whether there was a Mr. Williams in the plant.

Soon, a Mr. Williams appeared and I sold him a policy. Later, I sold Mr. Johnson a policy.

— *Ellen M. Putnam, CLU*

The only really successful way I've heard of selling insurance en masse was during the war. The Captain was trying to explain to his company of young men about government life insurance.

"Men", he yelled to the company standing in front of him at attention, "your Government makes it possible for you men to have $10,000 of life insurance and it costs you $5.00 per month out of your pay. Anyone who wants it step two paces forward."

Not a man moved.

The Captain tried again. "It's only $5.00 a month, men. That's very cheap for $10,000 for Mom if you should get killed. Now, anyone who wants it — step lively — two paces forward."

Still no one moved.

The Sergeant stepped up to the Captain saluted and said, "Excuse me, Sir, I think maybe you aren't explaining it right to them. Sir, would you like me to take a try at it?"

"Go ahead Sergeant, I'm certainly not doing very well."

"Yes Sir!" Then turning toward the company he said, "Now listen you guys, anyone who has this insurance, if he gets killed the government has to pay $10,000. Now the Government decides who goes up to the front where the shooting is and who stays back in the cushy jobs behind the lines. If you were running the Government, which guys would you send up front? Now everyone who wants this insurance, take two steps forward."

"Company — ee — halt!"   — *John O. Todd, CLU*

Charlie Peckham, my first manager in New York, lived in Connecticut. He once called on a rancher and tried to convince him to buy life insurance to provide income for his wife, but no sale. As Charlie was leaving, he noticed a beautiful horse owned by the rancher. Charlie, a horseman, praised the horse's beauty. The rancher glowed. Charlie asked him, "On your death, wouldn't you like to see the horse cared for and fed in the style to which he's become accustomed?" The rancher said, "Yes". Charlie discussed the horse's life expectancy and what it might take to feed and care for him. He sold a life insurance policy on the rancher to cover the horse's needs but not one cent for his wife.

                                   — *Edward J. Mintz, CLU*

As a home office sales trainer, I was working with a new agent in Abilene, Texas during his first week in the field. We were using the old *You'll Earn A Fortune* procedure and we had called on a pretty successful used-car sole proprieter who was a friend of my trainee. When we reached the point where my agent asked his prospect how much money he could save, per month, if he really wanted to, the prospect replied, "One hundred dollars." This young agent-trainee stopped and looked at this well-fixed used-car dealer, with a serious, quizzical expression on his face, and after some time said, "Can you really save $100 a month, or are you just ...ing me?" Needless to say, this angered the prospect to the point we never were able to get the interview back on the track.

                                   — *Howard O. Kemper*

As a new agent in the life insurance business I was very eager to make presentations and close sales. I had memorized every word of a new mortgage cancellation presentation and was just waiting for the opportunity to try it out on a "live" prospect.

One morning, after making a few unproductive phone calls, I decided to wear off some shoe leather making cold calls. On my very first call I hit "pay dirt". A very nice woman answered the door and, after my introduction, invited me in. Upon entering the home she introduced me to her husband, who nodded his head politely and smiled as he sat in his easy chair.

After the introduction she asked me if I would like some coffee and cake. Not wanting to offend her I replied, "Yes" and she excused herself to the kitchen.

In my eagerness to make my new presentation I began speaking to her husband. Before I knew it I was giving a terrific presentation. As I pointed to the charts and asked the questions, I would look at the husband for some acknowledgement. He smiled and nodded affirmatively and I continued. Just as I was about to ask the closing question the lady of the house returned from the kitchen with coffee and cake in hand. She stopped, listened for a moment, then laughed so hard she dropped the coffee and cake. Confused, I inquired as to what was so funny. Regaining her composure she said, "Honey, you're wasting your time. My husband is deaf and didn't hear a word you were saying." I was so embarassed that I packed-up my sales aids, made my excuses and left. I had just made a terrific presentation to a man who could not hear a word of it. But it did teach me one thing — *always be sure that the prospect not only understands what you're saying but hears what you're saying.*

—*Mark S. Cappock*

A young agent, new in the business, was well-trained in the "art of getting a commitment". He asked his prospect, "Can you afford a dollar a month?" The prospect agreed. Then he asked, "Can you afford $100 a month?" and again the prospect agreed.

The young agent was not mentally ready for this response so he blurted out, "Well, I can get it for you cheaper."

— *John L. Wozniak, CLU*

LIFE ASSOCIATION NEWS

"It's seven o'clock, Fred. Time to get up and start making a little cheese in the rat race."

On an appointment one evening I arrived at 7:00 pm. and was greeted at the door by the man of the house. He informed me that his favorite program was just beginning on TV. I said I was there to speak with his wife concerning her insurance program. He excused himself and went back to watching TV in the living room. His wife was in the laundry room standing at the front of her washer and dryer. I saw her put soap in the washer. She joined me at the kitchen table, where I proceeded with my sales presentation.

Half-way through the presentation she got up and went to the washing machine. She again added soap. She returned not realizing that she previously had put soap in the washer.

I finished my presentation and was into my close when I happened to look up and saw soap suds foaming out of the washer. I proceeded to ask her to sign the application. Meanwhile, the soap suds where climbing up to the ceiling about a foot away behind the back of my client. I asked for the check and she paid me. The woman's husband came into the kitchen for a beer and to see what I had sold his wife and suddenly began shouting that half of the kitchen was covered with suds. The wife sprang to her feet and went looking for a mop. Her husband followed after her and they disappeared into the suds in an effort to stop the machine. About this time their two children ran in from outside, saw me sitting at the kitchen table and heard voices coming out of the suds. The kids laughed and played with the suds. After they lead their father and mother out of the suds we all had a great time laughing at the situation.

—Anthony T. Colombo

One time during my first year or two in life underwriting, about 1920, a brother of one of my college classmates referred me to a friend of his who had a good job in the telephone company. The man was married with several small children.

I called for an appointment and went out to his home one evening. He was very cordial, said how glad he was to see me, that he was a great believer in life insurance and had plenty for his family in the event of his death. He proceeded to tell me what he had; namely, $300 in the Maccabees, $100 in the Prudential, $150 in the John Hancock, $100 with his company, and $300 with Woodmen of the World. With great difficulty, I managed to sell him a $1,000 policy.

— Ellen M. Putnam, CLU

A woman called her insurance agent to question the advisability of purchasing a dread disease policy. Included in the discussion was the admonition that the policy benefit was restricted to cancer only which accounted for the low monthly premium.

The would-be policyholder, not to be dissuaded, asserted, "With my luck, paying the monthly premium will guarantee I'll never get cancer. I've never won anything in my life!"

— *Anonymous*

LIFE ASSOCIATION NEWS
"Your quotas for this year are very simple—sell more than you sold last year."

PRESLAR
LIFE ASSOCIATION NEWS

"I've decided it's about time this company
gets into some profit sharing."

LIFE ASSOCIATION NEWS

"It's disappointing, Fred, 16th hole already
and, we still haven't hit on a solution to increase the productivity of the office staff..."

Since I am strongly committed to the benefits of life insurance, it is important to me that my close friends and family are adequately covered. Of the three couples with whom my wife and I most frequently socialize, only the wife of a medical doctor was not insured. On each occasion that I mentioned the need for Federal Estate Tax liquidity to the doctor, he would say that his wife was superstitious and did not want any life insurance coverage.

On New Year's Eve the four couples went to an elegant restaurant. Marcia said to me, "Larry, will you please come by the house tomorrow to see me." This caught me somewhat by surprise and I asked why. She said, "I want to buy some life insurance." I have always made it a practice not to discuss business matters during social occasions and everyone knew that. I asked her why she brought the matter up at that particular time and she smiled and said, "I thought you might like for our friends to know of my decision."

So I continued, "Marcia, I have been recommending coverage for you for such a long time, why did you finally decide to do something about it now?" She told me that she and her husband had gone to see their attorney the previous day and the first thing he asked her was how much life insurance coverage she had. When she told him that she had none, he told her to contact her insurance agent to rectify this matter. This was the first time she had seen or talked to me since the meeting with the attorney the preceeding day. She was bubbling with excitement. I asked her why, after the number of times I had proposed life insurance to her, that she took his word and recommendation and not mine. She replied, "Larry, he told me to buy life insurance. You always asked me." This resulted in a sale of $100,000 of Ordinary Life insurance being placed on her life.

— *Lawrence G. Katz, CLU*

I approached an old high school friend about buying some life insurance from me. He responded by telling me that he was divorced, but if I could help him find a wife, then he would buy some life insurance. I happened to think of a nice gal that I knew back in Illinois, who I felt would make a good wife for him, so I gave him her name and said, "It's entirely up to you, John. You will have to do the rest."

John was very clever at writing letters and from his correspondence with her, got her to agree to meet him at Rapid City, South Dakota. Evidently, everything clicked over there because it wasn't long after that John approached me on being best man for his wedding. Not long after their marriage, I, of course, followed-up on the insurance proposition and John bought. He has also bought several times since then. They have three lovely daughters and have done very well together.

— *Jack Woods*

Years ago, when I'd only been in the business for six or eight months, I went to make a call on a young couple. I felt things were going along well through my presentation, but I kept getting warmer and warmer and finally realized that the temperature in the house must have been well over 80 degrees. This was not summer — I believe it was late fall — and the heat was on making the house that warm. I asked if they'd mind if I took off my coat. I did so and kept on going with my presentation and felt things were going very well. Finally, however, it got so warm that I simply felt ill yet didn't feel I had the right to ask them to turn their heat down or open a window. Unfortunately, I got to the point that I simply couldn't continue and asked if they would mind if I laid down because I didn't feel well. They were very sympathetic.

I laid down on the couch, the man's wife got me a glass of ice water and I took a drink or two of that. While I was lying on the couch I thought, what the heck, I might as well continue, so I just simply continued the presentation while I was lying on the couch with both of them sitting in chairs next to the couch. They were impressed with the presentation to the point they decided they wanted to buy the policy. I pointed to where my brief case was and had them bring it over to me. I pulled out an application form and gave it to them, and they promptly went over to the table and completed the application. Although I still wasn't feeling too well by the time I left, it made me feel a whole lot better leaving with a policy of $20,000 on the young man and the check in my brief case.

— *Richard D. Mead, CLU*

LIFE ASSOCIATION NEWS

"Look out world! Here comes Herman Fernwhistle!"

37

This comes from my Life Underwriting Training Council class many years ago. One of my classmates, a former used-car salesman, was at a kitchen table interview one evening having mixed success. Every affirmative reinforcing statement he made was getting a yes-yes from the wife — while the husband was shaking his head no-no. The agent was losing the sale and he knew it.

The telephone rang and the wife answered. The call was for the husband. When he returned to the table to sit down the agent got up and said, "Sir would you please change seats with your wife?"

When this change had been completed the wife asked, "Why did you ask us to change seats?"

The agent replied, "I wanted to get him out of the no-no seat and into the yes-yes seat."

The subsequent laughter broke the tension and the sale was made!

— Carl B. Rush, CLU

I was on an appointment and was completing an application for life insurance on a client's wife. We were approximately half-way through when there was a knock on the front door. The husband answered. There stood two policemen who talked with my client for several minutes. Following their discussion, the husband returned to the kitchen where he, in a somewhat shaken voice, announced that he had just been arrested and would have to go with the police. He apologized for any inconvenience this might have caused and left with them.

Obviously, all kinds of thoughts crossed my mind and I was wondering what kind of person I was dealing with. As it turned out, he had just received his 16th speeding ticket in the last 18 months and that all had gone unpaid. It seems he was having trouble observing the speed limit in his Jaguar.

He paid his fines and did without driving for a while but since then he has purchased a lot more life insurance. He still has his Jaguar, although he has learned to control his urge to speed.

— James S. Doyle, CLU

This is a true story of my second month in the insurance business.

I nervously presented a $10.00 a month savings plan to a young couple in their home. They liked the plan and said, "We'll take $20.00 a month of that." Not being experienced, I doubled all the figures on the proposal. The clients were pleased so I wrote the life application accordingly.

After returning to the office, I realized the extra $10.00 a month qualified them for a policy with a higher face value and cash value plus dividends. I ordered an alternate policy of the higher values.

Two weeks later the policies arrived so I called the clients to arrange a delivery appointment. They set a time the next evening and then told me an agent from Company X had come over and had said he could provide a better policy than mine.

The next evening I arrived at the client's home and proceeded to explain the better policy for which they had qualified. They were seated next to me on the sofa and had agreed it was exactly what they wanted. Just then the doorbell rang and the agent from Company X walked into the room. He sat down on the sofa where Mrs. Client had been sitting and proceeded to explain to Mr. and Mrs. Client how much better his policy was than my original proposal.

I was flabbergasted by his rudeness but let him go through his entire pitch. When he finished, I informed him the policy I had just delivered was much better than the one I had originally proposed and much better than the one he had just proposed.

I then told him I hadn't seen him at the local Life Underwriters meeting and asked him if he belonged to this association which promoted professionalism and education of all life underwriters. I knew he wasn't a member because at that time his company would not permit any of their agents to belong to the National Association of Life Underwriters. What he didn't know was that I was still not a member but had just attended my first Life Underwriter's meeting that day and had my membership application on my desk to be filled-out.

Mr. Client said he wanted to do business with an agent who belonged to a professional organization. The agent from the other company said he thought he might join the Association in the future. With that he left as Mr. and Mrs. Client joined me in a big laugh.

Everything turned out fine as I had restrained myself under great duress, the clients had received the best policy for their premium dollars and the Life Underwriter's Association received one dedicated member.

— *Morland G. "Mac" McManigal, CLU, CPCU*

LIFE ASSOCIATION NEWS

"Yes, Charley! As a matter of fact you did wake me out of a sound sleep . . . but that's okay."

40

On a cold, snowy night, after getting to a prospect's house I found him very indifferent. After struggling through some fact-finding and really getting nowhere, he finally laid this gem on me: "Look, I appreciate all your efforts and concerns, but I really don't need any more insurance. I got $5,000 worth with double *identity*." Without laughing, I got myself together enough to thank him for his time, wished him the best of luck, and off into the snow I went.

— *Theodore M. Provenza*

A 97-year-old man presented himself at the insurance office and said he wished to take out a policy on his life. He filled out an application but was very much annoyed when he was turned down.

"You folks are making a big mistake," he said, "if you look over your statistics you'll discover that mighty few men die after they're 97!"

— *Anonymous*

The insistent salesman had his prospect backed up against the wall. "Take out our accident insurance policy," he insisted.

But the prospect still had some fight left. "Why should I?" he asked defensively.

"Listen!" boasted the salesman. "One month ago a man took out a policy with us. The other day he broke his neck and we paid him $5,000. Now think. Tomorrow you may be the lucky one!"

— *Anonymous*

LIFE ASSOCIATION NEWS

"Say 'oink'."

This tale goes back almost 30 years when I was a young neophyte agent in North Carolina.

I had been in the business about two years, had become "a sophisticated programmer" about to embark on previously uncharted waters, and was about to enter the "Doctors' Market". I had gotten all the necessary facts and data on a previous interview and had designed a magnificent "Dollar Guide" type proposal. It consisted of 25 pages of charts, analyses, and recommendations. To top it off, the crucial interview was being held under very favorable circumstances.

Part way through the presentation the physician/client gave rather distinctive "buying signals". Undaunted, however, I continued to deliver the magnificent manuscript, page by page. At several other points in the interview the physician attempted to agree with the basic recommendations. This was much to my chagrin. I was a "pumped up, sophisticated estate planner" who thought this client had a heck of a nerve to even suggest my full presentation was unnecessary.

Thus, it was with some amazement (and amusement) that I heard my physician/client say at the end of the presentation, "Gee, that's great, Frank ... thanks ... but say, do you sell any plain old life insurance?"

— *Frank J. Brennan, CLU*

The first million dollar policy I sold occurred as a result of this situation:

The prospect, his wife and I were all seated in the living room with the various proposals spread out before us. I was explaining how a Section 303 would dovetail with his Estate Plan and he agreed and turned to his wife for her nod of approval. She concurred and I completed the applications for both to sign. At that precise moment we were having a typical spring thunderstorm and as a result all the lights went out. You can imagine my reaction. I continued talking for five full minutes, that seemed like an eternity, about the advantages of their purchase. With the lights still off Mrs. Prospect got up to find candles. She handed me one and I held this to furnish the light for the required signatures to be affixed.

— *J.R. Pegues, Jr., CLU*

YOU KNEW THE ANSWER

You smiled so tauntingly
As you walked toward me,

You asked so charmingly
As you stood close to me,

You waited patiently
While your eyes caressed me,

You knew intuitively
What my answer would be.

You spoke softly and lovingly,
Your dulcet voice enraptured me;

You possessed my mind completely,
Your lovely smile captured me;

Body, heart and soul collectively
You owned me.

You knew intuitively
What my answer would be,

"Of course I'll buy your insurance policy."

—Stephen J. Skubik, CLU

"Is There a Doctor in the House?"

One evening a new sales representative and I were in the home of a distinguished elderly couple. They were both retired school teachers and they owned a substantial amount of farm land which they wished to leave intact to their only son. I was there because they were contemplating the purchase of a sizable insurance policy on the woman. After we had discussed the underwriting requirements and the fact that a physical exam would be required, the distinguished elderly gentleman said, "If we decide to buy this insurance on my wife, which one of you two guys is going to give my wife the physical?"

— *Larry D. Petty, CLU*

LIFE ASSOCIATION NEWS

"You got one get well card from the office, one from our insurance man, and eight from various bartenders around town."

Governor Ronald Reagan of California tells about the time that he applied for an insurance policy and went to see a doctor for his medical examination. When the exam was over, the doctor told Governor Reagan that he was in very good shape. As a matter of fact, he was as sound as a dollar. Reagan said, "I almost fainted."

— *Stephen J. Skubik, CLU*

In Salinas, California my company hired a good looking, young doctor as a medical examiner. He went on a house call to examine one of my prospects, an attractive elderly woman named Mrs. B. The doctor said to her apologetically, "I don't usually examine a woman without my nurse in attendance". Mrs. B. put her hand on his, smiled at him warmly and said, "You don't have to worry about me, Doctor, I won't attack you."

— *Edward J. Mintz, CLU*

On a Sunday morning several years ago, I received a phone call from the wife of a client. The conversation started, "What am I going to do? How am I going to support my family? What's going to happen to our business?"

For ten years I had gradually created a life insurance program for this family by selling them additional coverage on six different occasions. However, I can assure you they were not easy sales; they were reluctant buyers.

I proceeded to ask her what happened. Although not hysterical, she was quite distressed, she said that she and Tom had gone to bed the night before and while they were hugging, she felt a large knot behind his ear. They rushed to the doctor who confirmed the presence of an obvious tumor and immediately scheduled surgery for the next morning.

"Larry, can you get Tom any more life insurance before tomorrow?" I assured her there was no way and to just hope there was nothing really wrong. The conversation ended with me saying my prayers were with her and asked her to keep me informed. A tumor the size of a golf ball was removed from behind Tom's ear. The good news was that it was benign. Three weeks later you could hardly tell that he had had an operation. Later I called Betty to set up an appointment to further discuss their life insurance needs. Betty replied, "We don't need more life insurance now. Tom is ok!" All I could think of was the humor in her comments.

I waited another ninety days before calling again. This time Tom would say that his wife was superstitious and did not want any life insurance coverage. I could not agrue with an emotional attitude where logic was of no avail.

Finally, I was successful in arranging an appointment to see the two of them. Tom asked me how much more insurance I thought he needed. My reply was that if he bought any amount less than an additional $100,000 of coverage, he was being unfair to his family and to himself. "How much would that cost?", he asked. I replied that it would be approximately $3,500.00 per year. With little hesitation he said, "Let's get that started." From my experience as a salesman, I knew something had to be wrong. This guy was not that easy! He signed the application and the medical examination was arranged. Sure enough, the company asked for additional information with specific emphasis on any heart trouble. Tom had undergone a complete physical examination without telling me about it. The findings indicated an extra heart beat where there should not have been one. The underwriting decision was a table eight rating.

The next meeting took place in Tom's office. "Larry, how could you do this to me? You have known for a long time that I needed more life insurance and I have been ready to buy it from you." It didn't take too much effort to convince him to accept the rated policy, since the next time he might not be able to buy it at all.

— *Lawrence G. Katz, CLU*

LIFE ASSOCIATION NEWS

"You've got to cut down on the blubber."

I had a client who tried to collect for maternity under the Supplemental Accident benefit on his hospitalization.

— *B. Leonard Critcher, CLU*

I had one client whose life insurance was rated because he had a mistress. I went to deliver the policy and told him the premium would be $300 more. He asked why. I told him the home office found he had a mistress and had rated the policy. He turned red as a beet, scowled for 30 seconds, reached into his desk, pulled out a check book, wrote the $300 check and said, "Hell, she's worth it!"

— *B. Leonard Critcher, CLU*

Recently told by a Master of Ceremonies at a breakfast for Minnesota legislators, sponsored by the Small Business Council of the St. Paul Chamber of Commerce:

As business owners, we sometimes feel like the young lady who sat on a bench, picking up a big sliver of wood in a very sensitive spot. Not able to remove it herself, she went to a doctor.

The doctor makes his examination, but observing that it would be illegal to remove the sliver, gives her a prescription. The young lady is very perturbed; she doesn't want medication; she wants relief ... she wants it out! And she wants to know why it's illegal.

The doctor responds, "It is illegal to remove redwood from the recreational area without first getting an environmental impact statement."

— *Herbert F. Mischke, CLU*

My district manager accompanied a trainee on an appointment and without much delay they arrived at a point of the close which can trigger indifference or an emotional response — questions about the prospect's health.

"So, let me ask you the $64,000 question," the district manager said. "How's your health?"

The prospect excused himself and returned with a stack of folders and papers which measured about eighteen inches in height. He then began to unfold a depressing medical history riddled with an anticipated declination from even the most liberal underwriter starting at page one.

After what seemed an eternity, my district manager and the trainee left the prospect's house, adding they would see what they could do but to not hold any false hope.

Before hopping in the car the district manager turned to the trainee and said, "Remind me to bring something the next time we come here."

"What's that?" the puzzled trainee retorted. "Do you mean a Classified Rate Book or text examples of people in similar situations?" he asked.

"No", the district manager returned rather indifferently. "Remind me to bring a shovel, because I don't think he'll be alive when we return."

— *Lawrence J. O'Brien*

One day the insured came to the office to pay her premium, but she didn't have her coupon book with her. I asked if she knew her policy number and the due date. The woman thought for a few seconds and replied, "Due date? I didn't even know I was pregnant."

— *LaVerne Terry*

It was my first night in the life insurance business. While sitting in my bedroom making phone calls for appointments, I contacted an individual who had been referred to me by a friend and I was informed that this particular person was in the process of building a home. Having called him and identified myself as a life insurance representative and having asked for the opportunity to visit with him, he informed me that he could not see me at this point because he had just gotten the "shingles". Well, being as smart as I am, I just put two and two together and realized that he was in the process of putting a roof on his home.

I replied, "I certainly hope that you got a good price on your shingles." To which he replied, "What is your name?"

"Tom McInerney," and again he replied, "Tom McInerney, you are really a dumb S.O.B.!"

I hung up the phone, went to the kitchen and told my wife that my general agent told me it was going to be a tough business. Of course, the shingles he was referring to were medical in nature and not that of construction material. I did, however, call the man back and apologized, and asked for the appointment. And would like to report to you a happy ending to a funny story, but I never did get to see him.

— *Thomas J. McInerney, CLU*

John McKenna arranged for me to interview a widow, Mrs. H. We were seated under the portrait of her late husband. She agreed to insurance on herself so that the business founded by her late husband could be continued after her death. She agreed to be examined that evening at her home. I asked John to see if he could get a doctor. He disappeared into the office and returned shortly thereafter to tell Mrs. H. the doctor would be at her home for the exam at 7:30 that evening. We left. I said to John, "Congratulations on getting a doctor that quickly." He said, "I don't have one yet." I was horrified. He told me not to worry. He stopped by a liquor store and picked up a bottle. He went by the doctor's home and although the doctor was having dinner he came to the door. John handed him the bottle and told him he was to examine Mrs. H. at her home at 7:30 that evening. The doctor agreed.

— *Edward J. Mintz, CLU*

Working with my first female agent proved to be a red-facing experience. One cold December night we were in the home of a young, small-framed divorced lady. Just the three of us, my well-endowed female agent and our small prospective client. My agent had done a fantastic job. She sold the client on the idea that she needed to purchase adequate life insurance to take care of her daughter in the event of the client's untimely death. I remember being so proud of my agent as she got the commitment and began filling out the application.

All was going well until my agent asked, "Have you had any cancer, tumors, or polyps", to which the client responded, "Yes, I had some benign growths removed from my breast." My young saleswoman replied, "So have I. Isn't that embarrassing to go into the x-ray room and flop your breast on that table so they can take those x-rays?" To which the proposed insured replied, "Sharon, mine aren't big enough to flop."

— *Larry D. Petty, CLU*

One evening while I was making phone calls to my clients I made this error: My client's wife was in the hospital, having given birth to a baby boy. We talked for a short time and as I was ending the conversation I remarked, "Be sure go give *my wife* your best regards!" I was sure glad he couldn't see my red face.

— *Jerry Larsen*

An agent was taking an application for a health insurance policy from Annie Calhoun who lived in the Mississippi Delta. The agent asked her, "Annie, have you ever been bed ridden?" Her reply, "Yes Sir! Hundreds of times!"

— *Bower L. Johnston*

While enrolling a group case, one older employee kept objecting to the "group plan". I was finally able to get him to sit down and tell me his objection.

"I have never been sick or in a hospital and if I do, I don't want all these people going with me."

— *Carl E. Meyering, MBE*

In my early years in the business I concentrated my sales efforts on young married couples and, as a result, sold more health insurance than I really planned to. Here's what happened:

Bill and Mary were newly married. Bill had a good job and they were planning a family. We discussed their health insurance plans and needs. They were sold on a program but Mary insisted the maternity benefits were not enough. She asked me to explain why. I was ready for this objection because I had heard it before and was schooled by our home office health department. So, very carefully, I explained that pregnancy was not a sickness and from that point of view the company really was being liberal. As we continued to review the benefits, Mary suddenly jumped up saying, "It can be an accident!" I agreed, but not for insurance purposes.

— *Bright Newhouse*

A brand new agent in the life insurance business walked into my office and noticed a BALL jar sitting on my desk. Curiously, he asked what it was for. My reply was that I was working on a group case and that was the specimen bottle for the group.

— *David L. Corrie*

LIFE ASSOCIATION NEWS

"I must be in terrible shape! The doctor said I was as sound as a dollar."

Anyone who has helped process health claims is familiar with the standard questions. You can imagine the reaction to the claim form received with the following answers:

Nature of illness: Pregnancy

Is claim due to sickness or accident?   Accident

If accident, state when and how accident happened: Saturday night in the den while watching *Gunsmoke*.

— *Phil Irby, Jr., CLU*

While working in the western North Carolina mountain town of Bryson City with special agent "Flash" Gordon, we began talking to the 60-year-old owner of the general store.

This man had large real estate holdings and our sale was for estate taxes. We recommended $80,000 but the store owner said, "I'll take $60,000 of that there policy."

After completing the application and getting a check to pay the annual premium, he said, "How old before a feller can't buy insurance? My daddy is 85, but he owns more land than me."

We said that 85 might be pretty old for insurance. The store owner then said, "Well, daddy probably couldn't pass the doctor anyway 'cause he was loading hay last week, fell off the hay wagon, and broke his leg in two places."

— *E.L. "Jim" Horton*

At Warner Brothers Studio I obtained an application for a personal life insurance policy on the life of a film director. The medical examination was scheduled for two days later, to be done in his cutting room at the studio. As part of the exam, a urine specimen was required to be sent to the home office of the company for analysis. The doctor handed the man a container to fill and the director headed for the men's room to comply. He must have changed his mind about taking the insurance between the time I took his application and the completion of the medical examination two days later, because on the way to the men's room he passed the laboratory where the film was processed. He stopped there, filled the bottle with distilled water, closed it, and returned it to the doctor who, in-turn, forwarded it to the home office medical department.

A week later I received a letter from the medical underwriter saying that the specimen had no specific gravity and, therefore, they couldn't insure him, because he was already dead.

— Frank Nathan, CLU

LIFE ASSOCIATION NEWS
"We get good coverage of all fringe benefits here but I still can't see the doctor the company hired!"

After an application was secured and the medical exam done, an additional urine specimen was requested by the home office. On calling the client, who was a college professor, I asked him to simply mail the urine specimen back to the home office. A short time went by and a second specimen was needed by the home office. Upon calling the professor I asked him if he sent in the first specimen and he in turn advised me that he certainly did. He assumed that I had wanted him to swallow the small pill in the container and then use the bottle. A doctor was immediately called to see if the preservative pill would have any ill effect. The doctor advised that no physical effect would occur.

— *Jerry A. Herzberg, CLU*

The story concerns the new agent who was selling like an old pro, but often forgetting that each case had medical requirements. To counter this absent-mindedness, his supervisor stated that from that point on, no new case would be accepted without a medical and urine sample.

This worked fine until the agent began getting absentminded again. The supervisor cracked the whip and stated the agent could not turn in any cases without the medical and urine sample. Later that day, the supervisor heard a knock on the door, and looked up to see the young agent standing at the door with a huge smile, about 20 pieces of paper and a large bucket.

The supervisor asked what the smile and all the material was for and the agent replied, "I'm going on my first group case."

— *Kenneth B. Cohen*

In the early sixties, I was working with the owner-operator of a log truck. I had written a life insurance policy on him and was writing one for his wife. In those days the application used to read, "If proposed insured has been hospitalized in the last five years, name reason for hospitalization, accident or illness, number of attacks, and dates." I asked the woman if she had been hospitalized in the last five years and she said, "Yes". I asked if it was an accident or illness, and if illness, number of attacks and dates. She said, "Pregnancy and it wasn't an accident and I was attacked hundreds of times ... he's a horny guy!"

— *Jack Boyer*

Claim Department

A veteran agent was startled one day when one of his clients walked into the office and demanded the money that he had coming from his life insurance policy. The agent asked him whether he wanted to borrow against it or whether he wanted to take the cash value.

"Neither," the man said, "I want the death benefit."

"But you're not dead," said the agent.

"Yes, I am," said his client.

Thinking that the man must have become unbalanced, the agent said, "Let me prove to you that you are not dead." Then he took the man's finger and pricked it with a pin, saying, "You know that dead men don't bleed, but you are bleeding. What does that prove to you?"

"That proves," said the client, "that dead men really do bleed."

— *Managers Magazine*

A couple of years ago, a death claim was returned for further information with the following from the home office: "Please have the deceased complete a new set of claim forms so that we can process this request."

— *Patrick V. Wippel, CLU*

Two gentlemen were living it up at the Riviera. One day while sunning themselves, one of them asked the other what business he was in. The fellow said, "Stocks and bonds," and asked what business the other was in. He too answered, "Stocks and bonds."

"How's business?", asked the first broker. "Oh, I'm no longer in the business, we had a fire and I was wiped out but I did collect $100,000 on my fire insurance."

The other said, "That's very interesting. I collected $500,000 on my flood insurance when I was wiped out."

The first broker then asked, "How do you start a flood?"

— *Stephen J. Skubik, CLU*

LIFE ASSOCIATION NEWS
"You can give me a new lease on life? Fine . . . will I be able to afford the payments?"

An agent handed a $25,000 check to a widow. "Just think, Mrs. Lurch, your husband paid only two premiums on this policy and I am delivering $25,000 to you. It just shows how wonderful life insurance is. After seeing how life insurance works, don't you feel that you ought to have protection on your own life?"

The widow pondered a bit, then replied, "I think I will, since my husband was so lucky with his."

— *Ken Schweiger*

A farmer whose barn burned down was told by the insurance company that his policy provided the company build him a new barn rather than pay the cash value of the barn. "If that's the way you fellows operate," the irate farmer told them, "you can cancel the insurance I have on my wife's life."

— *Managers Magazine*

LIFE ASSOCIATION NEWS

"Albert, are we in good hands or do we own a piece of the rock? "

I had an insured's son who came home from a late night date and parked the car in the driveway of their rural home. Early next morning the father went out to start the car to go to work and heard a terrible clang, bang, and squeal. Investigation revealed the farm cat had crawled up onto the warm motor the night before and the fan sucked him into the radiator — result ... one dead and strained cat and one ruined radiator ... paid under comprehensive.

— *Gene Prosser*

An agent attended the funeral of one of his clients and stopped by to see the widow and said, "I'm sorry that it had to happen, but at least he was a kind, loving, and considerate husband, who recognized his responsibilities and had you and the children foremost in his thoughts."

The widow listened until the agent finished and then said to one of her children, "Danny, go over and see if that is really your father in the coffin."

— *Jennie Larson McNulty*

About six months after receiving a $10,000 payment from her husband's life insurance policy, the woman reported that her husband was alive. The person who was found dead had robbed her husband and was later murdered with her husband's wallet in his pocket. It was a case of mistaken identity. Her husband had run away from her but now had returned and all was fine between them. The insurance company was delighted to hear this. They wrote the woman a letter asking that she return the $10,000. The woman replied, "I can't do that since I have donated the money to Traveler's Aid who found my husband for me."

— *Stephen J. Skubik, CLU*

Claims are normally the most serious part of the insurance business, but some humor creeps in every now and again. The following explanations were reportedly received by one of Prudential's divisions as reasons for submitting claims:

My wooden leg was broken.

A man hit me with a ranch (wrench).

Sickness on account of garter (goiter).

I was up a tree after a squirrel and a guy shot me.

An airplane hit the house and came in.

I was accidentally kicked in the stomach by a customary fooling around.

I broke my foot when I jumped from a 10-foot bank to get down in a ditch so I could get up a tree.

I dislocated my shoulder swatting fly.

Headaches and earaches caused by my guitar.

Band corns. Could not wear shoes. Had them removed by surgery.

Fractured 37 ribs in an accident.

I fell from the ceiling at home and I am nervous to work now.

It started with a cough and ended up with an appendectomy.

I had the flue with a small touch of ammonia.

Fractured jaw. Hit by a person who must have thought I was someone else.

Bad eyes and swell feet.

Suffered burns while holding shirt tail up over an open flame to warm his back.

Put a tire patch on Playtex girdle and it caused infection on right thigh.

A light case of severe flu.

Romantic Flavor (rheumatic fever).

I was crossing a street when a car hit my husband and I broke my left foot.

Getting on a bus, the driver started before I was all on.

An amateur fire-eater — blowing fire out of mouth — it backfired.

Foot broke out and began to run.
I have athletes foot on my hands.
I wake-up unconscious.
Doctor's diagnosis: "a heavy social drinker."

— *Anne Marie Maier*

A truck backed through my windshield into my wife's face.

The pedestrian had no idea which direction to go, so I ran over him.

I had been driving my car for four years when I fell asleep at the wheel and had an accident.

I pulled away from the side of the road, glanced at my mother-in-law and headed over the embankment.

I was on my way to the doctor with rear-end trouble when my universal joint gave way causing me to have an accident.

A pedestrian hit me and went under my car.

The guy was all over the road; I had to swerve a number of times before I hit him.

An invisible car came out of nowhere, struck my vehicle and vanished.

To avoid hitting the bumper of the car in front, I struck the pedestrian.

I saw the slow moving, sad-faced old gentleman as he bounced off the hood of my car.

The telephone pole was approaching fast. I was attempting to swerve out of its path when it struck my front end.

Coming home I drove into the wrong house and collided with a tree I don't have.

I collided with a stationary truck coming the other way.

I was thrown from my car when it left the road. I was later found in a ditch by some stray cows.

In an attempt to kill a fly, I drove into a telephone pole.

The other car collided with mine without warning me of its intensions.

A stop sign suddenly appeared where no stop sign had every appeared before.

I was driving through the field and hit a fire hydrant.

The other car attempted to cut in front of me, so I, with my right bumper, removed his left rear taillight.

— *Russell C. Reitz, CLU*

One agent told me that he wrote a fire insurance policy on a man's home for $100,000. As the man was signing the application he asked, "Now, if my house were to burn down tonight, what would I get?"

"Probably about two years," the agent answered.

— *Ken Schweiger*

Highland, Illinois has an annual Community Christmas party for children and Santa always bails-out of a plane and lands by parachute to pass out gifts. A few years ago, a side wind caught Ole Santa and he landed on top of a car, crashing the top, and breaking the windshield. After he was carted off to the hospital we got the claim under comprehensive, falling objects. Needless to say, it was a bit difficult to find the right words for the loss report and keep it in clear communication.

— *Gene Prosser*

LIFE ASSOCIATION NEWS

An insurance adjuster, after returning from the investigation of a fire, told his boss what had started the blaze, "Friction" the investigator informed him.

"Was it caused by something rubbing together?" asked the boss.

"That's the answer," the adjuster said tersely, "The fire was caused by rubbing a $3,000 insurance policy against a $2,000 house."

— *Jennie Larson McNulty*

The client, his wife and his CPA were present. At this session, I was developing many tax ideas that would be beneficial to the client's family and his business. We covered the death aspects that arise from a qualified plan and the advantages of a corporate recapitalization in the form of a holding company to benefit their children and grandchildren. Suddenly, the client jumped to his feet and with a broad smile and his hands up in the air exclaimed, "Gee, I can hardly wait to die to see all these wonderful ideas implemented."

— *Melvin L. Maisel*

ENGLEMAN.
LIFE ASSOCIATION NEWS

"And now a prediction on how we'll be doing this time next year!"

A buxom young lady was driving down a highway wearing a low cut dress when she drove by a barn that was on fire, and a hot ash blew in the window and down her front. My company paid her insurance under the medical-pay claim. The claim attracted much attention through all channels.

— *Gene Prosser*

A woman wearing an anxious expression walked into an insurance office one morning. "I understand," she said, "that for $5.00 I can insure my house for $1,000.00."

"Yes," replied the agent, "that is right."

"And," continued the woman nervously, "do you make any inquiries as to the origin of the fire?"

"Certainly," was the prompt reply.

"Oh," she said, and she turned to leave the office. "I thought there was a catch in it somewhere."

— *Jennie Larson McNulty*

A report of a broken left car door simply stated:

"I was driving down the street and thought the window was down so I signaled with my arm for a left turn, but it wasn't."

— *Gene Prosser*

LIFE ASSOCIATION NEWS

"He doesn't actually worship it. He says it's a symbol for incentive during working hours."

LIFE ASSOCIATION NEWS

"One question—how much do you want?"

LIFE ASSOCIATION NEWS

"You guys be just as liberal as you like. You're
the ones who will have to cough up my Social
Security!"

LIFE ASSOCIATION NEWS

"He can't see you today. The I.R.S. has a lien on his time."

LIFE ASSOCIATION NEWS

"He'll see you now, just stare into the camera . . !"

LIFE ASSOCIATION NEWS

"I'm transferring you, Winston, my analyst told me to get rid of my frustrations!"

LIFE ASSOCIATION NEWS

"The color is compatible, but the price
clashes with my take-home pay!"

"Well, what with the quarterly payments and
April 15th, I've come to believe the D.C. after
Washington means 'Demand Cash'!"

ENGLEMAN.

"Congratulations, Jones . . . it's your mandatory retirement day!"

"This is Slave-Driver to Gold-Bricker. I'm coming in and those business reports better be finished!"

"I thought I'd heard everything, but you're the first self-employed man I've ever met who hated his boss."

"The ol' man sure knows how to keep his men in line."

LIFE ASSOCIATION NEWS
"Happy birthday, from all the staff and most of petty cash."

ENGLEMAN

LIFE ASSOCIATION NEWS
"What do you mean that's your C.B. handle?"

"If you're a modern youth who rejects the value my generation placed on money you'll love the salary!"

"Oh, yeah? Well, my dad gets the prime rate at Chase Manhattan and Morgan Guaranty Trust!"

"It's refreshing to run into the truth once in a
while!"

"With your particular approach to work, Wool-
gate, do you ever arrive?"

We Get Letters ...

Below is a copy of a letter I sent to my company. The beginning of the story is in the letter, but the best is yet to come. We have a paramedic who does some of our exams, named Lydia, who is a sweet woman in her mid 50's. Before she came to examine my client, I warned him that he was going to have to prove to Lydia that he didn't have hemorrhoids. But, as I didn't know Lydia well enough to have determined if she would think this was funny, I never mentioned it to her.

Lydia always calls to verify that the medical has been completed. She asked me if there was anything peculiar about these people because they giggled throughout the entire visit, and she couldn't figure it out. I then related the history to her and she gave a little chuckle.

In the meantime, my client's wife had photocopied my letter to the underwriting department and hung it in full display in the office of their construction firm.

Gentlemen:

Regarding Mr. _____'s attached application for life and health insurance, please be advised of the following information. Mr. _____ has a disability income policy in force with Trans Pacific Life Insurance Company. The policy is modified to exclude any disabilities connected with hemorrhoids.

Mr. _____ informed me that he does not now have, nor never has had, hemorrhoids. There was some misunderstanding when the application was completed. Mr. _____'s father-in-law was present when the application was taken. The agent asked one of the health questions, and Mr. _____ said, "There's nothing wrong with him except that he's a pain in the ass." It seems the agent took this comment literally and entered it on the application as an indication of hemorrhoids.

— *Margaret R. Beck*

ENGLEMAN.
LIFE ASSOCIATION NEWS

The following is a letter sent back by a dentist in response to a claim department question as to how a certain procedure was carried out.

A charge of one stick of dynamite was placed through the left nostril and forced into the glabella. A detonator was attached with a 20-foot fuse. I then evacuated the entire office. The fuse was lit. When I returned to the office the foreign body was removed — so was the patient.

I trust this fully answers your question.

— *J. David Dukehart, CLU*

I received a reply to one of my direct mail letters for newlyweds from the Central Corrections Institute. I did not know the letter had been mailed to the institute. The prisoner gave the letter to his wife who promptly returned the reply to me. I called the wife and she said she would be glad to set up an appointment in 5 to 10 years.

— *John T. Carpenter, III*

Here are some excerpts from actual letters received in our home office from policyholders. Is it any wonder why our home office has trouble making a point clear or understanding what some people are trying to say in their letters?

I am forwarding my marriage certificate and my six children. I had seven but one died, which is on a half-sheet of paper.

I am writing to say my baby was born two years old. When do I get my money?

I am glad to report that my husband who was reported as missing is dead.

Mrs. Jones had not had any clothing for a year, and has been visited regularly by the clergy.

I cannot get sick pay. I have six children. Can you tell me why?

This is my eighth child. What are you going to do about it?

Please find for certain if my husband is dead. The man I live with can't eat or do anything until he knows.

I am forwarding my marriage certificate and my three children, one of which was a mistake, as you will see.

My husband got his project out two weeks ago and I haven't had any relief since.

Unless I get my husband's money soon, I will be forced to an *immoral life.*

You have changed my little boy to a little girl. Will this make a difference?

Please send money at once as I have fallen in error with my husband.

I have no children as yet as my husband is a bus driver and works night and day.

In accordance with instructions I have given birth to twins in the enclosed envelope.

I want money as quick as I can get it. I have been in bed with the doctor for two weeks and it hasn't done me any good. If things don't improve, I will have to look for another doctor.

I have been under a doctor since my husband lost his business two weeks ago.

I am very much annoyed to find you have branded my boy an illiterate as this is a dirty lie. I was married to his fater a week before he was born.

In answer to your letter, I have given birth to a boy weighing ten pounds. I hope this is satisfactory.

— *Anne Marie Maier*

LIFE ASSOCIATION NEWS

"That sign has decreased accidents among the ladies 100%!"

An insurance adjuster tells of a policy that was taken out in the name of Abraham E. Smith who lived in a small southern town. For five years the insurance company received the premium payments when they were due and then, without warning, they stopped. The company sent several notices and finally received this reply:

Dear Sirs:

Hope you all will excuse us. We can't pay no more insurance on Abe because he died last September.

> Your truly,
> Mrs. A. Smith

— Jennie Larson McNulty

Below is a letter I recently received from a real estate promoter:

A.L. Balfay, CLU
P.O. Box 822
Tyler, Texas 75710

Dear Mr. Clu:

It has come to our attention that a man of your status may be interested in our beautiful lake lots. This is a personal invitation to you, Mr. Clu, to come see our beautiful new development on Lake Palestine.

We would like for you to bring Mrs. Clu and all the little Clus with you to enjoy the outing and see this beautiful new addition...

— A.L. Balfay, CLU

Below is a letter that was received in the Underwriting Department. The names of the parties involved have been deleted.

Life Insurance Company

Post Office Box_____
Dallas, Texas_____

Attn: Dr._____, M.D.
    Medical Director

Dear Dr._____,

RE: Leroy_____

Mr. _____ is a living museum of pathology. I am enclosing a summary of his illnesses of one year ago from the College of Medicine, Richmond, Virginia. As you can see there are many doctors who have treated him.

The only reason I can see for insuring him is to establish a lottery for people disposed to betting to see how soon he will die.

I think he is a very poor risk. If I may be of further help, please let me know.

    Sincerely yours,

    William _____, M.D.

W_/ tfc
Enclosure

— A.B. Mirmelstein

President Levine is a very rare and very unique gentleman, and there is a story behind that compliment.

A few years ago, I shared a headtable at a dinner in New York City with Norman Levine. A few people were good enough to ask me to sign their programs, and in so doing, my pen ran out of ink. So, I borrowed Norm's. Well, a few years went by and the next time I saw Norm was in March of this year, when he came to the Oval Office to ask if I would attend his dinner.

After the meeting was over, I asked Norm to accept a pair of cufflinks as a souvenir of his visit to the Oval Office. Norm was very gracious about it. He thanked me, but declined the offer and said, if I didn't mind, he'd just like his pen back.

So, I gave Norm a pen and that is why I say he is a very rare and unique gentleman. How often do you meet anyone who ever got something back from Washington?

President Gerald Ford
NALU Annual Convention
Disneyland Hotel Convention Center
Sunday, September 21, 1975
Anaheim, California

— Norman G. Levine, CLU

"I interrupt this meeting to bring you a special back-to-work bulletin."

"In reference to your letter of the eighth . . ."

One incident, which I recently came across, shows how much inflation and the level of services performed by doctors has changed in the last 79 years.

In our files we found a letter written in 1900 by a doctor. We had asked him to examine a child for whom his parents had applied to Prudential for a life insurance policy. The doctor's witty description of the many difficulties he encountered in complying with our request is a real contrast with today's difficulties of even getting a physician to make a house call. He caps all of this off by indicating his fee is $.25.

Prudential Insurance Company   Loch Raven
June 8, 1900

Dear Sirs:

I did not think it essential to see this child on this particular occasion because I attend the family, had seen him recently and know his health to be good. I thought this ought to count far more than simply seeing a child once. Moreover, his mother told me that she could not prevail upon him to come in from the strawberry patch to see me — he was afraid I wished to vaccinate him or something worse.

However, in accordance with instructions, I made the trip of nearly six miles, winding up with several hundred yards through woods and bushes at the risk of getting my newly done up buggy scratched, and came upon the boy in the strawberry patch. I had barely time to get a good view of him before he turned and fled through the woods like a startled deer, the frantic commands of his mother yelling after him having no effect except to increase his speed, if possible. But I had complied with the letter of the law — I had seen him. And now I respectfully submit that the requirements of the case have been fully met and my $.25 fully earned.

Respectfully,
H.T. Harrison, M.D.

— *Martin D. Vogt*

My Last Will and Testament

A lady having her portrait painted was pleased with the artist's work. However, she asked the artist if he would paint a beautiful diamond necklace around her neck with matching earrings and a 10 carat diamond ring on her third finger, left hand. The artist agreed but asked the lady why she wanted such lavish jewelry on her portrait. She replied, "I want the woman that my husband marries after I'm gone to eat her heart out looking all over my house trying to find the jewelry."

— *Maurice S. Gilbert*

All of us in the life insurance business are indebted to my late business associate, James W. "Jasper" Wood, CLU. One of the founders of LUPAC, Jasper worked tirelessley as LUPAC National Chairman for many years until his death on July 19, 1978.

Jasper's LUPAC achievements, his multi-million dollar insurance production, and his active professional, community, and church life were the result of amazing mental and physical energy combined with the IQ of a genius. He also possessed a sharp, home-spun sense of humor which served him well in many a sticky sales situation, as the following true incident will attest.

It seems that Jasper and a prominent Nashville tax attorney had done a thorough, much-needed job of estate planning on a certain physician. They had undergone an exhaustive series of fact-finding interviews with the client, the client's wife, and the other financial advisors. A new will had been drafted in accordance with the client's emphatically-expressed wishes, new business procedures relating to his medical practice had been installed, and the additional life insurance needed had been applied for and issued.

The final meeting between the client, the attorney, and Jasper was supposed to have been simply a "housekeeping and paperwork" session: signing the new business documents, paying the balance of the insurance premiums, and executing the new will. However, the client balked with the pen in his hand: he apparently had changed his mind with respect as to how he wished, in the event of his death, to endow his wife of some 20-odd years. It soon became evident that he didn't feel quite so kindly toward his wife as the earlier interviews would have indicated — and of course, all of the detailed plans had been made on the basis of leaving the wife in pretty good financial shape. The attorney and Jasper began to see a lot of hard work going down the drain.

"I'm not so sure," the client kept saying, "that I want to leave her so well off and then have a second husband appear on the scene."

"You mean," said Jasper, with a deadpan expression, "that with all this money, she'd be fair game for the first silver-tounged devil who came down the pike?"

"That's absolutely right!" the client agreed.

"Well," Jasper answered, that famous grin appearing on his face, "that's exactly what *won't* happen if you do what we're recommending. You see, with all this money, she can afford to be a little more independent and choosey — and that way she's unlikely to have to marry such a sorry man a second time!"

— *Charles D. Nord, CLU*

LIFE ASSOCIATION NEWS

"Send all department managers in for further cost cutting suggestions."

LIFE ASSOCIATION NEWS

"The old gentleman says, 'Being of sound mind, I blew the whole wad on wine and women'."

I was having a conference with an elderly couple who had been clients of mine for a long time. We were reviewing plans for changes in their wills, as well as what we should do about minimizing taxes. Grace was in bed suffering from a terminal illness.

Well, we got down to discussing precisely what Grace should do with her personal effects. She made a few decisions about leaving some of her jewelry to a niece and a painting to a nephew. We then discussed what she would do with the rest of her personal effects.

Grace said, "Well, Ed, when I pass on, which definitely I am going to do, I think you should remarry and have someone to look out for you and that is just exactly what I want you to do. Now, Ed, your new wife can have that two carat diamond ring you gave me, as well as that gold bracelet and the amber necklace we bought in Poland. You just go on and give her those things. And that new set of golf clubs you bought me last year, give those to her too." Blushing Ed replied, "Honey, I couldn't do that. She's left-handed."

— *Harry Lee Hamilton, CLU*

LIFE ASSOCIATION NEWS

"We have nothing against jogging, Munsey,
but we'd rather you wouldn't do it on your way
to the office."

Man's Best Friend

For years I had been telling people that our particular health policy would pay for the accidental injury to their natural teeth, but would not pay for repair of cavities, etc. About three years ago I had an instance come up where I could prove that our policy would pay for accidental injury to natural teeth. When I was called to help fill-out the claim, the insured explained to me how the accident had happened that knocked out her two front teeth. During the entire time she talked the woman kept hiding her front teeth behind her hand so it wouldn't appear so bad. The story went like this:

The woman was feeding her dog, which was a rather large sized dog, and as she was feeding it she was bending over a large pan. Directly across from the pan was her table. The dog, being all excited about being fed, was running circles around her and came charging right up behind her and jumped up with both of his paws on her rear end. This, of course, tipped her forward and, not being able to catch herself, she bumped her mouth into the table dislodging her two upper front teeth. Since the dentist was able to take care of everything in good order the story had a happy ending, and she still chuckles about it a great deal.

— *Richard D. Mead, CLU*

About 20 years ago, shortly after I had moved from our Chicago agency to Denver, I used a lot of direct mail in my attempt to develop new clients. One of those who answered agreed to an evening appointment at his home which was in a new area about 10 miles from where I lived.

Once I was in the area, I had trouble locating the house in that this was a new development and some of the houses were not occupied. Because there was poor lighting, I had to get out of my car to read the street sign to determine where I was. The only problem was that I left my car door open and upon my return I had a German Shepherd in the front seat with me. He didn't seem too unfriendly, but I was not sure so I went around to the other side and opened the door so he could get out. It was then obvious he didn't want to get out so I thought maybe he would like a little ride and then would leave.

I drove around the subdivision a short while, stopped and opened the door, and again he didn't want to leave. I didn't especially want to push him, so I decided to take another trip. After four of these excursions, he obviously became tired of my driving, and the last time I opened the door, he stepped out.

I had a little trouble explaining to my prospective clients that I had to take a strange dog for a ride around the area several times before I could get to their house. In fact, I don't believe that I did any business with that prospect after that evening. I guess I felt the business was going to the dogs.

— *Jerry Stahmer, CLU*

INTERNAL REVENUE SERVICE

FILE

LIFE ASSOCIATION NEWS

"In my book everything that keeps me alive is a business expense! If I wasn't alive I wouldn't be in business!"

I was sitting across the desk from the President of a company. It was summertime. All at once a bee flew down the front of my dress but I tried to act as if nothing had happened. I leaned forward and tried to mash it but to no avail. Don't ever let anyone tell you a bee only stings once. When I found that I couldn't kill it without letting the man know what was wrong with me I said to him, "Why don't you think over the ideas I have presented to you and I will call you in a couple of days?" I made a quick exit and headed for the nearest restroom to slay the bee.

— *Ruth Russell, CLU*

Back about 40 years or so, Walker R. Crump, Assistant Manager, and I used to call on the farmers in northern Virginia. Crump and I had just sold a $15,000 Whole Life policy to a dairy farmer, accepted a prepayment and arranged for the exam.

We were getting ready to drive away when Mr. Crump belatedly thought of giving the farmer some band-aids, pin cushions, etc. I stayed in the car and Crump hurried into their inner yard to give them to the farmer. Before he could get out of the enclosed farmyard, two dogs hit him. A big collie knocked him down and a small dog ripped off one of his pants legs!

We generally planned these trips for three days. Since he did not have another pair of pants, we had to return to Richmond right away.

— *Clifton H. Robertson*

One evening I had an appointment with a young couple who had just bought a home in Bladensburg, Maryland. When I made the appointment, it seemed that 7:00 pm was a convenient time for all. Being a new agent, I set out for my appointment ahead of time so I wouldn't get lost and be late. It so happened that I had no trouble finding the address and arrived a half-an-hour early. The young wife greeted me at the door and invited me inside. Before I had time to explain why I was early, an enormous, black German Shephard, bearing his teeth and growling, came tearing around the corner. I managed to jump to one side. The young woman grasped the beast, apoligized, and locked him in the cellar. Still a little shakey, I managed a smile and tried to regain my composure.

I found myself being lead to a dimley lit living-room. The wife explained her husband was only a block away playing basketball with some friends, and was expected to be home in a few minutes. We began chatting about their new home, the neighborhood, etc. As we talked I glanced across the hall into the dining-room and noticed a large acquarium. It was about six-feet long. I asked what she had that would require such large aquarium and she exclaimed, "Oh, I have an Iguana. His name is Igore!"

"May I see him?" I asked.

"Certainly," she replied.

I peered into the glass enclosure, and much to my surprise, all I could see was a little tail sticking out from under a rather large rock. My eyes traveled beneath the aquarium and startled, I gasped, "Oh my, that isn't a Tarantula, is it?"

"Oh yes," the woman replied, "Henry is one of the largest of his species."

Henry was indeed large and I was happy to see there was a screen over the top of his pen. Now I glanced around this old house wondering what other exotic pet she may have hidden somewhere.

By this time it was 7:30, and no husband. She excused herself to run down the block to get her husband. There I was in this dimly lit house, on an overstuffed couch, in their living-room.

All of a sudden, I heard a rattle, rattle, rattle, *CRASH!* There was silence for a few seconds and then on the bare floors I heard a scratch, scratch, hiss, hiss! Around the corner of the dining room came the five-foot Iguana, hissing, his long claws scratching on the old bare floors, and his tongue jutting out from the Teranisour looking features. "Oh my God!" I said. He was headed right for me, and was not wasting any time about it. There was no exit other than the direction from which he was coming. Getting my wits about me as quickly as I could, my only recourse was to climb up on the back of their old couch, balance as well as I could, and raise my arms grasping my only weapon, which was the enormous Prudential rate book.

The Iguana was now about two-feet from me. I thought to myself there was a possibility that I could jump over him and make my escape out the front door. I was about to leap when the husband and wife entered the house. The wife came into the living room, to find me on the back of the couch in my attacking stance. "Oh," she exclaimed, "Igore, where have you been? I have been looking for you all afternoon!"

Well, she scooped Igore up in her arms and carried him to the aquarium. She no sooner put him in one end and he slithered out the other, up and over the glass sides, onto the floor and disappeared. I was in complete shock! It would be only a matter of a few seconds and I surely would awaken from this horrible dream!

The Iguana, it seemed, had been sunning himself on the windowsill behind the lower shutters. When the sun had gone down, the rattle, rattle was the Iguana climbing up the shutters, the crash was the Iguana falling to the floor, and well, the rest you know.

Exotic pets, a house of unexpected horrors, unusual circumstances, you may call it as you like. The German Shepherd I could adjust to. The Tarantula I could do without. The Iguana, I certainly didn't need.

The evening turned out to be a successful one. I was able to help this couple solve a need by protecting their home with mortgage insurance. After that evening, I was never, ever, frightened to go into any house, anywhere, anytime. Certainly in the future years of prospecting, there couldn't be another experience that I couldn't handle.

— *Barbara B. Brown*

LIFE ASSOCIATION NEWS

"Do you think you ought to yell at me in front of your plant like that, sir?"

About five years ago I was summoned to jury duty and sat in on a rape and assault case. After the trial was over, I received a phone call from two ladies who belonged to a Women's Study Club. The result of the phone call was to visit with these ladies in regards to self-defense against being assaulted by a stranger. Upon welcoming these women into my home, on a cold winter afternoon, we shared and talked about this type of problem and what I had learned in the courtroom which could be of help to other women in our community. I must also add that we had just acquired a new Siberian Huskie puppy who was tied-up outside on a chain attached to our garage.

After an hour of visiting and as the ladies were preparing to leave, I walked out to the car with them and, much to our wonder, the whole front of their car was completely destroyed. Our puppy had been playing and her paw had hit the front of the grill of the small compact car. The grill was made of a plastic substance which shattered all over the driveway. The headlights and turn signals were hanging by wires out of the sockets. The plastic rims to the headlights were laying on the ground and there, sitting in the middle, was our puppy wagging her tail and proud as a peacock. After much embarrassment and some laughter, I called our insurance agent and was informed that our homeowners insurance would cover the cost of the repair to the damaged car. The agent won the award for the strangest claim of the year.

— *Patricia A. McMahon*

I was working a housing development where every house in the neighborhood looked the same. I was making an early evening house call and as I waited for the door to be answered, a huge, friendly dog came loping around the side of the house. Well, that critter was about to lick my face, paws up on my shoulders, when my prospect opened the door. The dog then gleefully bounded inside.

It was not an easy presentation. That big animal kept racing from room to room, poked around in my open attache case, and jumped up and down on every chair and couch in that house. Finally, when the dog became so distracting that I could no longer contain myself, I took the risk of insulting my prospect and said, "Would you mind giving the dog some milk or something so we can go on with this thing." My client leaped at the opportunity to quiet the dog and fetched some milk.

Finally, with a little respite from that annoying animal, we were able to conclude our business. Happily, I made the sale.

Now, in post-sale euphoria, I became exceedingly friendly and commented to my "client", "What a nice dog you have."

He said, "My dog? I thought it was your dog!"

— *Murray W. Kronick, CLU*

LIFE ASSOCIATION NEWS

"Not that I want to contradict you, dear, but the computer tells me that you don't need bread until tomorrow nor eggs until the next day."

A very successful member of the Million Dollar Round Table from Des Moines, Iowa entertained a well-known United States Senator when the Senator came to Iowa to campaign for President of the United States.

As the insurance man was an avid deer hunter, he invited the Senator to go hunting with him. Early one morning they drove out to a farm owned by a client of the insurance man.

The insurance man told the Senator he would go ask the farmer for permission to hunt. The Senator sat in the car while his friend went to talk with the farmer. The insurance man told the farmer the Senator wanted to hunt with him and the farmer agreed to let them.

The farmer then told the insurance man he had a 21-year-old donkey that was on its last leg and that he couldn't get himself to put the donkey out of its misery. He asked, "Would you mind shooting the donkey for me?" The farmer pointed to the donkey standing by the barn. The insurance man agreed to shoot the donkey.

On his way back to the car the insurance man thought he'd play a trick on the Senator. As he opened the car door he pretended to be very angry. He told the Senator the farmer refused to let them hunt.

He then said, "Hand me my rifle. I'll show that so-and-so." He aimed his rifle at the donkey and shot him square between the eyes. The donkey dropped dead.

Just then the farmer's prize bull came out of the barn. The Senator grabbed his rifle and shot the bull dead, and said, "Let's get out of here."

The farmer ran toward the car shouting, "You shot my bull. You'll pay for this." The Senator denied he did it. He said, "I'm not a bull shooter."

Needless to say when the word got out to the farmers of Iowa that the Senator was a bull shooter, the farmers voted against him. And that is the reason why the Senator lost in Iowa.

The point of the story is: Iowa farmers don't vote for bull shooters.

— *John R. Carter*

In Southern Georgia, where I was born and reared, we used to go squirrel hunting early in the morning.

If you left home before daylight, walked out into the woods before the crack of dawn, and stood there under the hickory nut trees as the sun grew slowly in the east, you could shoot quirrels as they came to eat the hickory nuts.

On one particular morning two friends of mine walked into the woods among the hickory-nut trees just at the crack of dawn. As soon as it became light enough for them to see, they started shooting squirrels out of the tops of those trees.

They were shooting a large number of squirrels and were stacking them up just like cord wood at the base of the tree when all of a sudden they looked up — and lo and behold there stood the game warden!

One of the hunters stood still, but the other started running — with the game warden in close pursuit.

He ran through the woods and the game warden followed. He ran down the hillside, with the game warden right behind him. He ran through the bushes and brambles and tore his clothes almost to threads, and the game warden stayed right behind him.

Down at the foot of the hill he ran through a creek almost waist deep, but the game warden didn't lose a foot on him.

The hunter splashed through the creek and out on the other side into a bramble patch where not only his clothes were torn more, but his skin was cut and bleeding as he came out of the bushes on the far side. But the game warden followed him right through the brambles and out the far side.

The hunter continued to run and he ran up the hillside. The game warden was huffing and puffing, but he stayed right with him. The hunter couldn't gain on him but neither could he outrun the game warden.

Finally, as the hunter reached the top of the hill, he stopped. The game warden came running up to him and demanded to see his hunting license.

The hunter slowly reached in his pocket, pulled out his hunting license and handed it to the game warden.

The game warden looked at it and was completely bewildered.

He said, "Please tell me why you did something like this. Look at you, your clothes are torn off, you're cut and bruised and bleeding. And look at me — my uniform is completely ruined, the briars and the bushes and the brambles have scratched me so that I will be weeks healing. Why did you do all this? All I wanted was to see your hunting license, and you had one all along."

The hunter looked him straight in the eye and said very calmly, "Yes, but my friend — he didn't have one."

— *Raymond King, CLU*

"I'm here to spur you on in case you falter!"

OLD BLUE

A few years ago there was a well-known court case held in the small county where I was born and reared.

On the morning this case started, the door opened at the back of the courtroom and in came a man that was to be the first witness of the day.

He had a cast on one leg. He had a big bandage on his head. On one side of his face was a long red gash that you could tell had recently healed. He had a brace on his back. One arm was carried in a sling. He walked with the aid of a crutch and the assistance of his wife.

She helped him down to the front of the courtroom and placed him in the witness chair. Shortly after he was seated, the jury was sworn in and the judge started this particular case.

The defense lawyer rose from the defense table and, as only a lawyer can do, pointed a long finger at the witness and shook his finger and said, "Is it not true that on the day of this accident you told the state patrolman that you were not hurt?"

The old man sitting in the witness chair looked at the defense lawyer, then turned his head and looked at the jury and then turned his head and looked toward the judge and finally said, "Do I have to answer, Judge?"

The judge responded quickly, "Yes, you must answer the question."

The old man said, "Well, Judge, let me tell you why I made that decision. This is what happened:

"It was early that frosty morning and I was driving my mule and wagon down the road and sitting right there beside me was Old Blue, my favorite hound dog.

"I had just come over a hilltop and had gotten about half-way down the hill on the other side when I heard a car coming over the hill back of me. I looked back over my shoulder and saw it comin' over the hilltop — traveling like a bullet! I've never seen a car travel so fast!

"Well, Judge, I got my mule and wagon as far out of the road as possible. In fact, my old mule was down in the ditch and the two right wheels of my wagon were in the ditch — but this car just came flyin' down the hill, slammed into the back of my wagon and tore it into a million pieces!

"Judge, that wreck knocked Old Blue, my favorite hound dog, way up in the air and over the fence and out in the field ... knocked my old mule way down the road in the ditch on the right-hand side ... and knocked me across the road and into the ditch on the other side.

"I don't know how long I laid there Judge, but the next thing I remember was that I heard another car coming over the hilltop making an awful noise. I finally was able to turn my head and look toward the hilltop and just as I did, I saw a state partrol car come over the hilltop. The siren was going and the blue light flashing and it came flying down the hill and slid to a stop in a cloud of dust right side of me.

"The state patrolman opened his door, got out of the car — and he must have been six feet, six inches tall! He didn't say anything — just looked around, hitched-up his pants, and began to see what had happened.

"Now Judge, Old Blue, my favorite hound dog, was hurt bad because that wreck had knocked him way up in the air and over the fence and out into the field. And of course Old Blue was moaning and groaning and making a lot of noise.

"This state patrolman heard him, walked down in the ditch, stepped over the fence, walked out into the field, and looked at Old Blue.

"He didn't say a word. He just took out a big pistol and shot him twice right through the head.

"Now Judge, my old mule was hurt bad too, with two broken legs. He of course was making a lot of noise and was moaning and groaning ... and of course this state partrolman heard him.

"Again, he didn't say a word. He just walked back through the field, stepped over the fence, walked across the ditch, walked up on the side of the road, walked down to where my old mule was laying in the ditch, and without a word, shot him twice right through the head.

"Now Judge, it was about that time that this state patrolman finally noticed me laying in the ditch on the other side of the road. He swung around toward me with that pistol still in his hand, the barrel smoking and lookin' like it was three inches across!"

" 'And how do you feel?' he asked me."

"Well Judge, it was at that point that I reached the decision — to just jump up and say, 'Mister, I feel just fine.' "

— *Raymond King, CLU*

It seems that when the Creator was making the world, He called man aside and bestowed upon him 20 years of normal sex life. Man was horrified.

"Only 20 years?"

But the Creator wouldn't budge.

Then He called the monkey and gave him 20 years too, but the monkey said he only needed 10. Man spoke up and asked if he could have it and the monkey said yes he could.

The Creator then called the lion and gave him 20 years. The lion only wanted 10 so man asked if he could have it and the lion roared, "Of Course!"

Next came the donkey. He, too, was given 20 years, but like the rest, said 10 was enough. Of course, man was greedy and asked for the extra 10 years, and the donkey said yes.

This explains why man has 20 years of normal sex life,

10 years of monkeying around,

10 years of lion about it and

10 years of making an ass of himself.

— *Anonymous*

"We, the People ..."

Often times it is pointed out to insurance people how important action is — doing something rather than just talking about it. However, I've always felt that well-thought out action makes more sense than moving too quickly or "shooting from the hip." One of my favorite stories makes this point fairly well.

The story concerns a young man who was cruising down the highway on his motorcycle on a brisk morning. The wind was blowing and it was rather chilly outside. He was wearing a leather jacket but all of the buttons had been torn off. Consequently, the jacket did not give him much protection from the elements. He conceived the idea that if he put the jacket on backwards, the wind would tend to cause the jacket to cling to his body and keep him warmer. Everything worked out quite well until he wrapped his motorcycle around a tree. An Irish cop who investigated the accident wrote in his report as follows: "The victim seemed to be doing pretty well as I approached him. But by the time I got his head straightened around, he died."

— *Lewis C. Yount, CLU*

Some years ago during my company convention in Palm Springs my wife Dorothy and our daughter, Marie, then 6, were sitting by the pool. It was Texas Week and a 19-year-old Miss San Antonio came by, modeling a black satin bathing suit with fringe on top. I told Dorothy, "That's a pretty bathing suit; you should get one like it." My wife said, "Even if I did, I wouldn't look like that in it." Then my daughter pinched me and said, "You shouldn't look at that girl that way." I blinked because I didn't think my drool was showing, and said, "It doesn't do any harm to look." My daughter replied, "Dad, I wonder what you look like to her?" This was a low blow. "What do I look like to you?" I asked. Said Marie, "You're old and bald and fat."

— Edward J. Mintz, CLU

LIFE ASSOCIATION NEWS

"Two o'clock there's a sales meeting, three o'clock you have a board meeting and four o'clock is your appointment with the hair stylist!"

Each time a young farmer visited his elderly grandmother in a nursing home he brought along a bottle of fresh milk. And, he would always put a little brandy in it. One day grandma said to the young farmer, "Grandson, do me a favor, please."

"Sure, just name it," he said.

"Whatever you do, young man, don't ever sell that cow!"

— *Ken Schweiger*

A client of mine struck oil on his farm in Oklahoma, and one of the wells caught fire. He called Red Adair who wanted a quarter of a million dollars to put out the fire. Then he called a local company called Indian Joe who agreed to do it for $20,000. At the first gray light of dawn, Indian Joe's 1932 flat-bed truck appeared on the top of the hill with 20 Indians in full war paint dancing in the back of the truck. The truck headed towards the flaming oil well at ever increasing speeds, finally smashing into it and spilling the Indians in all directions. With shirts, feathers, and hair on fire, whooping and hollering, they finally put out the fire and Indian Joe came to my bug-eyed client who presented him with a $20,000 check, saying, "I have never seen anything like that! You guys are amazing. What are you going to do with the money?" To which Indian Joe replied, "First thing we are going to do is fix the brakes on that truck."

— *Marshall I. Wolper, CLU*

I'd like to pass along a true story about Mississippi's legendary Senator Theordore G. Bilbo. He was known as quite a lady's man in the 1930's, thrived off hecklers at the political rallies, and was quite a controversial, colorful figure in the state for many years. He served one term as Governor of the State of Mississippi and three terms as Senator. The story goes like this:

Senator Bilbo was a native of Poplarville, MS, which is in the southwest corner of the state. During his campaign for senator, he was speaking in Tupelo, MS, located in the northeast corner of the state. One of his opponents had really gotten on him as a lady's man and accused him of having "kept" a woman in Hattiesburg, Meridian, Laurel, Jackson, Greenwood, and even Tupelo, while his poor, old wife stayed down in Poplarville.

Bilbo, as usual, rose to the occasion. As Bilbo got up to speak back to his opponent, he said, "Now, it may be true I have a "kept" woman in Hattiesburg, Meridian, Laurel, Jackson, Greenwood, and right here in Tupelo. And, it's also true I still have my dear, little wife down in Poplarville. Now, I want to ask you ladies and gentlemen a question: If a man can keep a woman in all them places and still stay married to a lovely, little lady in Poplarville, he's got to be man — a real man — now ain't that right?"

— *Charlie Crumbley*

While calling on a client at his home one Saturday, his five-year-old son bounded into the room. The father called him over and said, "Johnny, this is Mr. Hanlon, the nice man who sends you a birthday card every year." After a moment in deep thought, Johnny brightened and exclaimed, "Oh, that must be the one with no money in it!"

— *Joseph T. Hanlon*

*"Sit down, Lionel, and we'll go over your new
management techniques goof-by-goof!"*

At a Million Dollar Round Table convention I was
talking with Ben Feldman and Ben Silver. A young man
approached with his hand out in greeting. "Ben," he
said cheerfully. The genial Ben Silver stuck out his
hand. The young man brushed by him as though he
didn't exist and shook Ben Feldman's hand. Ben Silver,
also a big producer, was completely deflated although
we have laughed about it many times since.

— *Edward J. Mintz, CLU*

The little boy ran up to his mother on the beach and
asked, "Can I go in swimming?"

"Certainly not, it's much too deep and there's a cur-
rent strong enough to drown anyone."

"But Daddy's in swimming," the boy pleaded.

"That's different ... Daddy's insured."

— *Ken Schweiger*

During the first few weeks of my training in the life insurance business, I came across a prospect who was extremely religious, probably to the point of being a fanatic. I didn't realize this when I first started talking to him but as we were discussing various ideas and the need for insurance I asked him what insurance policies he had at the time. I also asked the amount of the insurance and who the companies were.

He took one look at me and after a long pause said, "I have Eternal Life."

My mind was racing — Eternal Life? Crown Life? Life of Georgia? Life of Virginia? Eternal Life?

About the time I was about to ask him how much the premiums were, I realized that he was telling me he was never going to die.

— *F. Grice Whiteley, CLU*

An agent asked his client, "Are you going to stick with the Straight Life?"

The client replied, "Heck no, I like to fool around, chase women and all that stuff!"

— *Tom Fitzgerald*

"My taxi driver gave me a counterfeit twenty dollar bill," said the husband to his wife.

"Oh my, let me see it," said the wife.

"I can't, I paid my insurance premium with it," replied the husband.

— *Stephen J. Skubik, CLU*

My favorite agent was telling me the other day that his wife was storming mad and complained, "That new cleaning woman must have stolen two of our towels."

"Well, some people are like that," the agent said. "Which towels were they?"

"The new ones," his wife said, "the one's you brought back from the hotel in Miami."

— Ken Schweiger

The year I was honored as Top Club President with New York Life was also the year my wife, Dorothy, was pregnant and couldn't travel with me to all the conventions. Wherever I traveled on speaking engagements I was given the best hotel accommodations. At the Broadmoor in Colorado Springs I was given a five-room penthouse suite. I called Dorothy and described the accommodations, saying, "It's a shame they have to go to waste." She said, "Make sure they do."

— Edward J. Mintz, CLU

While trying to find the Lodge Apartments on a night appointment during a driving rainstorm, I unknowingly turned into the wrong complex. After driving around I realized that I was obviously in the wrong place, a low-rent project. Nevertheless, at this point, I felt it best just to go to an apartment and ask for directions. When the door opened, I peeked out from under my dripping umbrella and said, "Are these the Lodge Apartments?" A wide grin spread over his face as he replied, "Yas Sar, some of these apartments is quite large!"

— Phil Irby, Jr., CLU

ENGLEMAN

LIFE ASSOCIATION NEWS

"Your husband phoned, he said to pick up a quart of milk and a loaf of bread on your way home!"

LIFE ASSOCIATION NEWS

"It's not as though we're asking for another coffee break! All we're asking for is a lousy 20 minutes for Transcendental Meditation to turn out better work for the company."

"... And the Winner is ..."

On the day of our last luncheon Charlie Siragusa, Jr., CLU, President-Elect of the Rochester Life Underwriters Association, was being honored and had as his guests his wife, Edie, a son and daughter-in-law, as well as his father. His father was very proud of Charlie and also proud of the fact that he was attending the luncheon, having been a life agent years ago.

You could just tell by his erect posture and bearing that Charles Siragusa, Sr., was immensely pleased with himself and his family. This fact was not lost on our out-going president, Mark Smith, CLU.

On the way out of the parking lot Charlie, at the wheel, stopped by for a moment as Mark hailed him. Mark leaned into the car window and said, "I'm surprised you let the kid drive!"

It broke us all up — including Charles Siragusa, Sr.

— *Catherine Covey*

A few years ago Gordon Rose, of the American College, asked that I have previewed in local high schools their new film, Huebner's *Human Life Value*. The object was to get the students reaction and to possibly include the film in our film library for loan to high schools in the states of Washington, Oregon and Idaho, as a part of our Consumer Education Program.

Upon receipt of the print I called a teacher at one of the leading high schools asking that she preview the film at a class on a Monday. I also said that I would like the student critiques by Tuesday as I planned to

LIFE ASSOCIATION NEWS

"I'd like the businessman's lunch, only I'm just a woman executive—so don't hold the food up for cocktails."

ship the film to Portland. The instructor had previously used several films in our collection on insurance. The instructor inquired as to the name of the film, and I replied the film was *The Human Life Value* produced by the American College of Life Underwriters. After some hesitation she replied she would be glad to show the film, *but,* due to it's controversial nature she would have to get permission from the local school board. Thus, she would be delayed in showing the film. I tried to allay her fears as to the controversial nature of the film. However, she insisted that any film dealing with the "unborn child" would have to be previewed.

In other words, we in the insurance industry often find that we speak a language misunderstood by the general public. Due to the publicity on abortion she misunderstood entirely the title of the film ... *The Human Life Value.* Human life value in insurance means how much money you are worth to your family, alive.

— *Clifford C. Halfhill, CLU*

This story involves one of the great story-tellers in all the land — Marv Kobel, NALU's Vice-President of Public Relations.

Marv was breaking me in as the brand new NALU Committee Chairman for Public Relations, and had scheduled a trip to New York City for a briefing by HIAA and ACLI ad programs, to be followed by a meeting in Hartford with the PR Chairman. My wife and I flew to New York where we had reservations at the Waldorf-Astoria Hotel, thanks to Marv.

We arrived at our room and I knew someone had made a big mistake at the hotel. But, rather than admit anything, I remained silent. The bellman showed us through this absolutely baronial suite. Besides huge ceilings, the suite had a large livingroom with chairs and sofas for well over 30 people — in just the livingroom — all genuine antiques!

LIFE ASSOCIATION NEWS

"Hi there! I'm here to put your company in
the black!"

In addition, there were two enormous bedrooms, a huge wet-bar, complete kitchen and dinette, dressing rooms, walk-in closets, several fireplaces, and two bathrooms bigger than any public restroom I had ever been in.

As soon as the bellman left, and after I toured all this splendor, I called Marv's room. I knew damn well NALU didn't pop for these kind of suites for anyone, let alone a committee chairman. When I told Marv about what must be a horrible mistake, he just laughed.

"Enjoy it, turkey," he said, "I told my old buddy, the hotel manager, that you and Arline had just gotten married! He and I went to the University of Wisconsin together."

"But Marv," I protested, "this is going to cost a fortune!"

"Enjoy, enjoy," he said. "They are only billing us for a small room at the lowest commercial rate."

I may live a hundred years and go to some swell places — and I've been to quite a few already — but nothing will ever compare to the seldom used Presidential Suite at the prestigious Waldorf-Astoria Hotel. I now know how the other half lives and I liked it very much. Even for just one day, a day I'll never forget.

— *George A. Corkum, CLU*

Recently in Tyler, Texas we had an honorary plaque made for one of our Chartered Life Underwriters. In large letters at the top was C.L.U.

When this was taken to the art shop to be framed, the owner of the shop bristled-up and handed it back and said he didn't want to have anything to do with the Civil Liberties Union. It took a little explaining to get him to frame the plaque for us.

— *A.L. Balfay, CLU*

LIFE ASSOCIATION NEWS

"This different drummer you march to in relaxing
and not working too hard . . . does he happen to be
our competitor?"

The Home Office

In 1926, before the founding of either the American College or the Million Dollar Round Table, one of the first pieces of whimsical humor I heard was about two old friends from a small town in North Dakota who met on the street one day in Minneapolis.

"Hey boy — it's great to see you — what are you doing for a living here in the big city?"

"Well," answered the other, "I'm selling life insurance — but please, when you get back home, don't tell my mother. She thinks I'm tending bar!"

— *John O. Todd, CLU*

LIFE ASSOCIATION NEWS

"I suddenly find myself in my peak spending years, sir. When can I expect my peak earning years to arrive?"

A bishop and a general agent both arrived simultaneously at the heavenly gates. The general agent was ceremoniously ushered in, but the bishop was told to wait outside. Miffed at this treatment, the bishop was further incensed when he peeked in and saw the excitement caused by the general agent's arrival. A special choir was hastily assembled to do him honor, a golden carpet was spread for him to walk upon, and angels flitted hither and yon strewing beautiful flowers on him and on his path. It was an astonishing reception thought the bishop, with a touch of bitterness.

Eventually, the excitement died down and the bishop was told to come in. There was no golden carpet, no choir, and no singing angles. Upset, the bishop asked St. Peter why he had not gotten the same treatment as the general agent.

"Don't let it bother you," said St. Peter. "You see, bishops arrive here routinely, but this is our first general agent."

— *Managers Magazine*

If you are going to be dealing increasingly with Washington Bureaucrats you should have the following interpretation of some of the standard clauses that you will find in letters:

"Matter is under consideration," really means "I never heard of it."

"Matter is receiving preferred consideration," really means "I'll have a shot at finding the file."

"You will recall this matter," really means "I know darn well you have forgotten it, or never knew, because I'm sure I don't."

"This urgent matter is hereby transmitted to you," really means "You hold the bag awhile — I'm tired of it."

"Please take appropriate action," really means "Do you know what to do with it? I don't."

"Kindly expedite your reply," really means "For Pete's sake, try to find the papers."

R. Edwin Wood, CLU

LIFE ASSOCIATION NEWS

"You are going to get stuck with another luncheon check."

A flowering introduction is like dividends; it's not to be considered as a promise or guarantee of results.

— *Jack M. Williams, CLU*

Two former insurance agents were hoboing in Colorado when they stopped along the river cutting through the canyon. The trout were jumping, the birds were singing, the sun was shining; it was indeed a lovely day. One of the former agents said, "Hoboing isn't all that it's cracked up to be. I remember the cold nights in the park, the lousy food at the mission, the railroad detectives chasing me and the dirty looks that people gave me."

The other hobo said, "Well if you don't like being a hobo, why don't you go back to selling insurance?"

"What?" asked the disgruntled hobo. "You don't think I'm going to admit being a failure?"

— *Stephen J. Skubik, CLU*

The Personnel Department was astounded to find they had a 105-year-old retiree — and his wife was still living too!

The personnel man said to him, "We're happy to find you in excellent health and look forward to sending you many more retirement checks. Incidentally, to what do you attribute your longevity?"

"Well young man, when we were married 85 years ago," he said, "my wife and I agreed that if I lost my temper, she would remain quiet. If she lost her temper I would take a walk."

The old-timer rolled-up his pants leg to his knee and said, "Have you ever seen bigger leg muscles than these?"

— *Ken Schweiger*

At the company's annual convention, an agent sat at the dinner table listening to his general agent make a speech. The general agent espoused many principles of good human relations that he himself did not practice and finally the agent turned to the woman on his right and said, "I hate that man."

"Why," exclaimed the woman, "that is my husband!"

Taken aback for just a moment, the agent said glibly, "That is why I hate him."

— *Managers Magazine*

A very successful agent with my insurance company used to give all of his new policyholders a calendar. When his manager asked the agent why he gave his policyholders a calendar, the agent replied, "To remind them when to pay their insurance premium."

— *Stephen J. Skubik, CLU*

I once had to fly to see a policyholder in Fresno, CA. There were no commercial flights to there from Salinas so I chartered a plane. On the way back the pilot said, "You can press the seat button, the seat goes back, and you can rest and relax." I did and fell asleep. When I awoke I looked at the pilot beside me. He was asleep with the plane flying through the air. I shook him and when he opened his eyes, I said, "Shouldn't you be awake?" He answered, "The plane is on automatic pilot." On future flights my secretary gave me No-Doz pills for him.

— *Edward J. Mintz, CLU*

One of our new agents handed me his weekly activity results report. He did not have a good week of sales. As I started to look at the report, he said, "Before you say anything, just remember ... the Hope Diamond was once a piece of coal."

Thomas C. Karrasch, CLU

Statistics are like bikini bathing suits — what they reveal is interesting, what they conceal is vital.

— Jack M. Williams, CLU

A prosperous young general agent fell in love with a rising actress of great talent and beauty. He wanted to marry her, but being a cautious man, decided that before proposing he would get an investigative report on her. In due time, the investigator's report came back. It said the actress had an unblemished past, a spotless reputation, and friends and acquaintances of the best repute. "The only negative we have to report," concluded the investigator, "is that Sue is often seen around town with a cynical, suspicious jealous insurance man."

— Jennie Larson McNulty

At the home office of an insurance company the general manager called in the department managers to discuss a problem concerning a very sexy but stupid secretary. The boss asked the department heads for a show of hands of those who had not dated the secretary. Only one of them raised his hand. The manager said, "Okay, Bob, you fire her."

— Stephen J. Skubik, CLU

Some years ago, when I was young and very green, I was testing the use of an audio-visual for my company.

I had an appointment one cold winter evening with a young farmer. When I got there, some of his hogs had gotten out and getting them corraled was our first order of business.

When we finally got to the house, we found his wife had gone to a church meeting leaving their young children without any supper.

I had a hostile prospect, but, having nowhere else to go, I plunged ahead with my AV presentation. When the film was finished I dutifully kept my silence.

The farmer asked, "How much does that cost?"

I said, "What, the machine?"

He said, "No, the damned insurance!"

Without much help from me, he did buy (the insurance) and it's still in force.

— *Thomas A. Crowe, CLU*

LIFE ASSOCIATION NEWS
"I used my management by objectives technique on our manager."

Delbert, when asked, "How is the insurance business?" responded with, "I am going to starve to death." Delbert's brother-in-law, who had gotten him into the insurance business said, "Now Delbert you have to be positive." Delbert said, "O.K. I am *positive* I am going to starve to death."

— *Gene Akin, CLU*

I met an actuary's daughter — I know she was an actuary's daughter because she gave me her cash surrender value.

— *Jack M. Williams, CLU*

The yacht was sinking off the California coast, so the owner radioed for help. The Coast Guard radioed back "We are on the way ... what is you position ... we repeat ... what is your position?"

Came the reply, "I'm the local general agent for Ajax Life, and please hurry."

— *Managers Magazine*

My brother used to tell people that I was perfectly sane until someone said "insurance" ... then I was off like the old fire horse when the bell rang.

— *Jennie Larson McNulty*

The phone rang, the receptionist answered and the call was for me. She buzzed my office and said that a Mr. Schuster was on the telephone, and I said, "Gee, I don't know a Mr. Schuster."

The receptionist said, "Well, it's a Mr. Victor Schuster, and he asked for you specifically." So I said okay and accepted the call. I proceeded to bluff my way along to see if it was something that I had forgotten and after a couple of minutes of conversation, and three Mr. Schuster's later, the man said to me, "No, no, no, this is not Mr. Schuster, this is Victor's Shoe Store." You can imagine my embarassment. Not only didn't I get the name correct, which wasn't my fault, but I then had to try and bluff my way along giving the impression I knew who Mr. Schuster was all the time.

— *Eleanor J. Sivillo*

On a joint interview with a new agent I was introduced to the president of the company. After the agent gave the president a long-winded presentation of my background as an expert, the president stood up and said, "He's too big a man for me." I assured him with my definition of an expert: "one who speaks on a simple subject in a confusing manner, but so convincingly you think the confusion is yours and not his." He laughed and we proceeded to make the sale.

— *Edward J. Mintz, CLU*

Our staff had handled a meeting of company officers at which a guest speaker had mentioned Eskimo practices in regard to their senior citizens. He recounted that when an Eskimo is too old and feeble to be anything more than a burden, his family takes him out to die by "exposing him to the elements."

We sent a tape recording to the typing pool to have the talk transcribed. The typist had obviously never heard of this practice, but she rendered it as best she could. In her version the Eskimos took the senior citizen out and "exposed him to the elephants."

— *Bart Yohn*

A woman applying for a job with a general agent for an insurance company asked if the GA would pay for her life and health insurance. The GA said that he would but that he would deduct the premium from her pay. The woman applicant protested saying, "The last company I worked for paid for my life and health insurance, paid for my pension and profit sharing plans, gave me three, fully paid weeks of vacation and gave me a bonus at the end of each year. The GA asked the woman why she left the company that was so good to her. She replied, "The company went bankrupt."

— *Stephen J. Skubik, CLU*

A young agent went to lunch with a prospect and the prospect decided upon the "Businessman's Special". The agent ordered two slices of plain toast and a glass of water.

The prospect asked, "What's the story, are you on a diet?"

"No," replied the agent, "on commission."

— *Sumner Rodman, CLU*

LIFE ASSOCIATION NEWS
"Can he call you back? He's working on a new incentive program."

My cousin Lou, who is in the casualty insurance business, related a story to me. He told me about being awakened around 2:00 am by the ringing of his telephone. The voice over the phone said, "Lou, this is Max."

"Yea, Max, what's wrong?"

"Lou, I have lost my raincoat."

"Why did you call me at this time of the morning to tell me about this?"

"Lou, you have my coverage and I want to know if I am covered or not."

"How much is your raincoat worth?"

"I would guess about $75.00."

"All your records are at my office but I think you have $100 deductible, so you are not covered."

"Thanks, Lou", and he hung up.

About twenty minutes later the telephone rang againg and the client awakened Lou for the second time. "Lou, It's Max again."

"Yea, Max, what do you want this time?"

"Lou, I just want you to know that I found my raincoat!"

— *Lawrence G. Katz, CLU*

The President of an insurance company called in his comptroller and told him that it was discovered that he had embezzelled $50,000 and for this he was being fired. The President said that because the company could not stand the bad publicity, the comptroller would not be prosecuted, but he should just quietly pack his gear and leave. The comptroller said, "Mr. President, I now have no more need to steal from the company. Why hire someone else who won't be able to live on the salary you pay him?"

— *Stephen J. Skubik, CLU*

ACTUARY — a person who would rather be totally wrong than practically correct.

— Jack M. Williams, CLU

I was transferred from the Canadian Head Office to the Prudential Corporate Office in April, 1977. When we purchased a home I called the local Prudential agent to obtain some homeowner's insurance.

As the agent began writing the application he asked where I worked. I told him that I worked for Prudential. He was a little surprised but pleased to serve a fellow PRU employee. Then he asked where my wife worked. I responded that she also worked for Prudential — she had also worked at the Canadian Head Office and was given a job in the Comptroller's Department in the Corporate Office. The agent could hardly believe it.

When he finally asked about the mortgage I told him it was with Prudential (as part of the relocation package). He was half-stunned and half-elated. He said the underwriting area wouldn't *dare* turn this one down. He smiled through the rest of the process of writing the application.

— Ross Rennie

A manager, when asked why he required all his agents to keep their hats on in the office, replied that it was to remind them they had no business there.

— Jennie Larson McNulty

At a New York Life convention in Miami Beach, I invited my mother, who lives nearby, to attend a cocktail party where the fabulous Ben Feldman was present. I said, "Mother, this is Ben Feldman, the worlds greatest life insurance salesman." My mother's face fell. She said she thought I was the world's greatest. Ben, being very diplomatic, said, "Mrs. Mintz, everything I know about the insurance business I learned from your son." Said my mother, triumphantly, "I'm glad you admit it." Later, she was sitting near the swimming pool at the hotel. A woman behind her was talking about the great Ben Feldman. Hardly turning her head over her shoulder, my mother said, "Everything he knows about the insurance business he learned from my son."

— *Edward J. Mintz, CLU*

ENGLEMAN.

LIFE ASSOCIATION NEWS

"I'll bet I can guess who prepared your resume; this is an exact copy of the one they gave me when I was looking for a job!"

"Sir, may I speak to you as a human being?"

After 20 years in the life insurance business, I find myself busy enough that I am often a few minutes late in keeping appointments. I didn't realize that I had a reputation for running behind on my appointments, however, until I recently arrived 12 minutes late for an appointment and was met with a scowl by the office manager. When I asked why she was upset, she replied, "Because you're usually at least 20 minutes late, and we're not ready for you!"

— *James E. Griffith, CLU*

I was riding with an insurance agent on a four propeller plane and we were scheduled to land with only a few minutes to spare before my speaking engagement. Well, one of the engines went dead and the pilot says, "Don't worry. We've lost power to one of the engines but we will land only about 15 minutes late."

My friend was starting to worry and fidget when another propeller went dead. On came the captain with another message ... another 15 minutes delay.

Just as the pilot finished that announcement the third engine went dead. The agent looked at me and said, "One more engine and we'll be up here all day!"

— *Roger A. Brownell*

At one of our company conventions I was greeted by George B. who said, "I want to thank you for your book." I smiled my appreciation. Then he went on. "I had it with me when I got on the plane at Nashville. It took off and we went through one of the worst storms I can remember. The plane was bouncing around so I took out your book and started reading it. It immediately put me to sleep and I slept through the entire storm. Better than sleeping pills ... no night table should be without it." Needless to say George B. is not one of my favorite people.

— *Edward J. Mintz, CLU*

A janitor answered the insurance office telephone while cleaning after the office was closed. An excited policyholder began asking questions about his insurance policy. The janitor replied, "Sir, when I said hello, I done told you all I know."

— *Thomas C. Karrasch, CLU*

Four or five years ago, a policyholder moved to Macon, GA, from Savannah. He phoned our office to have his policy transferred so our clerical office sent in the request to the home office. When his semi-annual premium became due the notice went to his old address. He phoned again and again and each time our office sent in the request. The same thing happened several times more. Each time he would call asking for the transfer and each time we sent in the request. After about the sixth or seventh time, he phoned and said, "It happened again! Let's try once more and if we can't get it changed, I'll just move back to my old address in Savannah!"

— *J. Sam Warren, CLU*

LIFE ASSOCIATION NEWS

"Incidentally, Mr. Bremson—Did you know the word 'dictation' stems from the word 'dictator'?"

After talking interminably about himself and his accomplishments, the loud and insufferable super agent said, "I'm a self-made man, too."

"You knocked off work too soon," said his general agent.

— *Managers Magazine*

It seems as though Old "Tom" was going out on the town every night and causing quite a fuss. Finally, the Old Maid had Old Tom fixed. He still goes out on the town, but now he goes out as an "advisor."

— *Jack M. Williams, CLU*

"What's your name?" asked the agency manager of the recruit applying for an insurance agent's job.

"Richard Nixon," replied the recruit.

"Richard Nixon, that is certainly a well-known name," the manager said.

"Yes sir, but it sure didn't do me any good when I was trying to sell used cars."

— *Stephen J. Skubik, CLU*

LIFE ASSOCIATION NEWS

"The man we're looking for should be aiming steadily for my job—but not too accurately while I'm still around. . . ."

P.S.

THE FOOLPROOF COLLECTION SCHEME

When I sold my wholesale distributing business in the mid-fifties to enter the life insurance business I was unable to dispose of a couple past due accounts which ran into several thousand dollars each. They were not only past due but virtually uncollectible, for my two former cutomers were not only very broke but even less anxious to pay for a dead horse.

My coincidental exposure to the miracle of life insurance gave me an inspiration and I conceived an ingenious device to collect my two bills. I made a deal with each debtor not to press him for collection and to waive any interest on the account if he would agree to buy an endowment policy from me to cover the debt, naming me as beneficiary to the extent of the bill and owner of the policy as well. We even put double indemnity in the deal, so that if the poor guy happened to die in an accident, there would be sufficient proceeds to liquidate the indebtedness with a like amount left-over for his family

By setting up the endowments over a reasonable period of time, we were able to keep the premiums down in the $20-25 a month range, and the fellows seemed willing and able to pay that much to get their bills out of the way. Had they died along the way, by any means, I would get my bills paid.

One of the deals paid out on schedule; the other chap took bankruptcy after a couple of years and I got nothing; but at least I had my two years of commissions.

The idea seemed so good at the outset and had been accepted so readily by my two impoverished debtors, that I thought other people might find it equally work-able. So I put a classified ad in the paper stating that I had a foolproof method of collecting bills where other means of collection might have failed. Most of the replies I received involved large numbers of small bills, which of course did not lend themselves to my scheme. But there was one which looked promising.

It involved a single account of quite adequate size to make my method workable. I contacted the creditor, explained my system, got his acquiescence and all the details. It seems the bill was owed to him from a brother who managed a grain elevator in a small northern Montana town with the incongruous name of Big Sag. The town was so small that it was not even on the map and I had difficulty finding anyone who could direct me to the place over virtually nonexistent dirt roads.

But I was young and persistent in those days and I made my way to this isolated place and found my man, right where he was supposed to be, tending to his chores in the elevator. As it turned out the grain elevator was the only building in town. I explained my mission and that's where the plan went all to pieces. It seems there was a bit of bad blood between this guy and his brother and the elevator man not only denied owing his brother a red cent but grew increasingly hostile as the conversation proceeded.

About this time I noticed, with some apprehension, that he was wearing a large pistol in a holster on his belt; I decided this was not such a good case after all, and beat a hasty retreat. As I left the elevator I heard a couple of pistol shots and it didn't take me long to clear out of that town. I later figured out that he had probably been shooting at rats in the elevator, but be that as it may, I am no longer in the collection business, and I have never been in another grain elevator!

— *Jerome H. Kohn, CLU*

"I used to be the toast of the town. Then I ran
out of bread."

"It's the boss. He wants to feed your
brain some data . . ."

The insurance agent said: "I can't quit my company. I am married to it."

His wife replied, "Great. Sue it for non-support."

* * *

When you look at the requirements of the regulators and the training level of some salespeople, you have some sympathy for the Duke of Wellington's feelings when, upon reviewing his troops, he was overheard to remark, "They might not frighten the enemy, but they scare the hell out of me."

* * *

The best way to stress the importance of precision in a beneficiary designation is to tell your policyholders about the man who wrote to his life insurance company asking that the $100,000 of his life insurance proceeds be paid to his widow only on the condition that she remarried — so he could be absolutely certain that at least one guy would be very sorry he died.

* * *

The thoughtful man will be hesitant in offering advice as to what the manager should know about his job, on the hunch that many aspects of agency management are like sex, where achievement is superior to knowledge.

* * *

When an actuary and a general agent go into the bar, the general agent always comes out sadder and the actuary wiser.

* * *

It is an actuarial equivalent of sorts that those who are most fond of getting you straightened out have no real sorrow seeing you screw up.

* * *

In selling the home office, "Sir, you are a genius!" is the only power phrase you will ever need to know.

* * *

Knowing the Socratic method of analysis and inquiry is not only valuable — it is easily mastered. Like this: I ask myself, "Why did I do that?" I answer myself, "It beats the hell out of me."

— *The Cragg Commentaries*
Ernest E. Cragg, CLU, FLMI
Farnsworth Publishing Co.
Rockville Centre, N.Y., 1979

LIFE ASSOCIATION NEWS

'I certainly question how young Farbestar did at Business Administration."

THE JACKPOT FLYER

For a few years during my company's illustrious history, they used to send out a little flyer with each direct billed premium notice. The message on the flyer varied from month to month — one month it would talk about retirement income, the next about mortgage insurance, etc. On the reverse side were boxes to be checked to indicate an interest in, and to request more information about, one or more of the various products. There was also a place to fill in your name and address.

The scheme was abandoned after several years as not producing results commensurate with its cost. But one morning, while it was still in full swing, an associate of mine and I decided to head up into the ranch country. On our way out of town we took a precautionary pass by the post office in case there was some last minute piece of mail demanding immediate attention.

As I came out of the post office I said to my associate that we had really hit the jackpot and showed him one of these little flyers which had come in that day's home office packet. It was from a chap in a nearby town, right on our intended route, and three of the boxes were checked; the fellow was interested, he said, in mortgage insurance, disability income, and wife insurance!

"If we can just find this guy," I said to my cohort, "our day will be made, even if we never catch up to one rancher."

In less than an hour we had reached the community where this man lived, and although it was just a tiny village, even by Montana standards, we had some difficulty locating our triple-barrelled prospect. We finally pinned him down in a ramshackle house at the far edge of town. Upon entering this dwelling, somewhat gingerly I might say, we found our individual. He turned out to be almost as unprepossessing as his abode. But he was alive, and he had three needs, so we started in.

It seems he had bought a modest hospital confinement policy during a bank solicitation we had carried on in his community some time previously, but had closed his account. His policy had been shifted over to direct billing and the flyer he had sent in was the first such thing he had ever seen.

Always inclined to be orderly, my associate and I took his needs one at a time in the sequence he had listed them.

"Now about this mortgage insurance," I started out. "We need to know how much of a balance you owe on your place here, and how long it has to run." (Who

148

would have loaned money for this disreputable shack defied the imagination, but we had to ask the questions.)

"Oh, I don't owe a cent on the place," he said. "It's free and clear."

Scratch one need. So my buddy launched into area number two.

"When we write disability income coverage," he explained, "we can only cover a reasonable percentage of a person's normal earned income, and the rate depends on how hazardous an occupation he is in. So we need to know what you do for a living and how much money you earn each month."

The reply came loud and clear. "I'm on welfare and I don't earn nothin'."

Fire three!

"OK", I said, taking over the interview from my non-plussed companion, "let's talk about some life insurance on your wife — how old is she?"

"Wife, hell," he said, "I ain't married."

We were two disappointed agents. It shows you should never get your hopes up until you have cased the joint. One couldn't help but feel sorry for this poor character — obviously he had never been exposed to flyers before, and he thought when you sent your money in your were supposed to check some of the boxes, so he had checked with a vengeance.

You know, it's really not surprising the company abandoned the flyer project.

— *Jerome H. Kohn, CLU*

THE GREAT MISSOURI HELICOPTER CAPER

A decade or so ago in the modest-sized Mississippi River town of Cape Girardeau, Missouri, there was an agency for a prestigious eastern mutual company headed by a fellow who, for the sake of anonymity, I will call

Bill Smith. Cape Girardeau is the county seat and the site of the annual county fair. Bill's agency had, for many years, operated a booth at the fairgrounds where fairgoers were invited to register and guess the number of beans in a jar, the weight of the hog on display, or what have you. Bill's agents manned the booth and for their effots received a share of the registrants' names for use in prospecting. And in addition, were privileged to visit with these people as they stopped in at the booth.

The agents tired of this project after a number of years, complaining that manning the booth was both boring and time-consuming. They also said they were not only getting the same names year after year but that soliciting among this group was becoming less and less productive. And so they asked Bill to either give up the booth or come up with a new idea.

It so happened this particular year a helicopter pilot was coming to the fair with his machine (helicopters were more of a curiosity then than they are today), and was going to take people on short rides over the surrounding area for $10. Bill and his agents decided to capitalize on this event, so they gave up the fair booth and contrived a scheme to offer a free helicopter ride to anyone who would buy a policy the week before or during the fair. They then placed an ad in the paper communicating their offer.

The ad had immediate results. The insurance commissioner called and informed Mr. Smith that he was offering something of value as an inducement to purchase insurance. This constituted rebating under Missouri law and the ad must be cancelled forthwith. It had already run two days when the commissioner's call came, and before the newspaper got around to implementing the stop order it had run a full week.

So, like many other ideas, this one went sour. However, as Bill later explained, the result was not entirely bad.

"We only sold one policy during those two weeks," he related, "and the fellow who bought it had not even seen

the ad and would have no part of the helicopter ride."
But the helicopter pilot did a land office business, and
every time he circled the valley, Bill went on to say, everybody in Cape Girardeau figured Bill Smith's agency
must have sold another policy.

— *Jerome H. Kohn, CLU*

LIFE ASSOCIATION NEWS

*"Phone call from a Mrs. George Filstrup for a
bum named George Filstrup."*

LIFE ASSOCIATION NEWS

"Where are you going to settle down when you retire?"